DISCOVERING THE PAST

SPECIAL NEEDS SUPPORT MATERIALS

THE MAKING OF THE UK

TEACHERS' RESOURCE BOOK

COLIN SHEPHARD   ANN MOORE

JOHN MURRAY

Societies in Change
   Pupils' Book ISBN 0-7195-4975-2
   Teachers' Resource Book, 2nd edn ISBN 0-7195-7041-7
Discovering The Making of the UK
   Pupils' Book ISBN 0-7195-7052-2
   Teachers' Evaluation Pack ISBN 0-7195-7053-0
The Making of the UK Special Needs Support Materials
   Picture Pack ISBN 0-7195-7044-1
   Picture Pack Workbook ISBN 0-7195-7226-6 (single)
                         ISBN 0-7195-7233-9 (pack of 5)
   Teachers' Resource Book ISBN 0-7195-7043-3

The authors and publishers would like to thank all the schools
which trialled these materials, and would particularly like to thank
Barbara Brown, teacher adviser for special educational needs in
Warwickshire, for her helpful advice and comments.

Photographs are reproduced by courtesy of: The British Library
(p.37), Mary Evans Picture Library (pp.58, 60, 128 right),
The Hulton Deutsch Collection (p.73), The Mansell Collection
(pp.88, 121, 123, 136, 179), The Museum of London (p.152).

© Colin Shephard and Ann Moore, 1995

First published 1995
by John Murray (Publishers) Ltd
50 Albemarle Street
London W1X 4BD

Illustrations by David Anstey, Art Construction, Sarah Blair, Ann
Moore and Chris Mutter

Layouts by Amanda Hawkes

Typeset in 14/18pt Quorum Book
Printed in Great Britain by St Edmundsbury Press, Bury St Edmunds

A CIP catalogue record for this book is available from the
British Library

ISBN 0-7195-7043-3

THE SCHOOLS HISTORY PROJECT

This project was set up by the Schools Council in
1972. Its main aim was to suggest suitable objectives
for history teachers, and to promote the use of
appropriate materials and teaching methods for their
realisation. This involved a reconsideration of the
nature of history and its relevance in secondary
schools, the design of a syllabus framework which
shows the uses of history in the teaching of
adolescents, and the setting up of appropriate
examinations.

Since 1978 the project has been based at Trinity
and All Saints' College, Leeds. It is now self-funding
and with the advent of the National Curriculum it has
expanded its publications to provide courses
throughout Key Stages 1–3, and for a range of GCSE
and A level syllabuses. The project provides INSET for
all aspects of National Curriculum, GCSE and A level
history, and also publishes *Discoveries*, a twice-yearly
journal for history teachers.

Enquiries about the project, INSET and *Discoveries*
should be addressed to the Schools History Project,
Trinity and All Saints' College, Brownberrie Lane,
Horsforth, Leeds LS18 5HD.

Enquiries about the *Discovering the Past* series
should be addressed to the publishers, John Murray.

Series consultants
Terry Fiehn
Tim Lomas
Martin and Jenny Tucker

Contents

Introduction

◆◆◆◆◆◆◆◆◆◆◆◆◆◆◆◆◆◆◆◆◆◆◆◆◆◆◆◆◆◆◆◆◆◆◆

All too often the history diet offered to pupils with special needs has consisted of crosswords, word-searches and 'gap-filling'. SHP's special needs support materials, on the other hand, have been developed to meet a specific demand from schools for materials that have all the hallmarks of SHP's 'real history' approach – in which pupils investigate issues and explore sources for themselves, and reach their own conclusions – but which at the same time recognise the very real problems some pupils have with the language of written source material and the unstructured nature of some historical tasks.

These materials have been developed by a team of writers and special needs advisers. They have also been trialled in a number of schools around the country. The result is a set of flexible and innovative strategies which aim to:

■ motivate pupils to find out about Britain in the sixteenth and seventeenth centuries, by developing their historical skills and understanding at an appropriate level
■ give all pupils access to this important core unit
■ add variety to the teaching of **The Making of the UK**.

The materials consist of this Teachers' Resource Book, with more than 200 largely photocopiable pages, and a companion Picture Pack, which contains 18 full-colour, large-size pictorial sources, together with a wide range of suggested activities using the pictures. The Picture Pack activities can be photocopied from the accompanying teachers' notes, or a separate workbook is available. All in all these materials provide several 'pathways' through **The Making of the UK** which will suit a wide range of classroom situations.

The three pathways

■ Pathway 1 is for pupils who have severe difficulties with reading. Through the Picture Pack they can receive a 'minimum entitlement' **Making of the UK** unit – through the use of pictorial source material alone.
■ Pathway 2 is for lower-ability pupils who can, nonetheless, cope with a certain amount of carefully targeted reading and writing. The Picture Pack and the differentiated worksheets, games and stories in this accompanying Teachers' Resource Book together provide a flexible alternative to using a class textbook. Indeed, this pathway can operate independently of any textbook and does not require users to have classroom sets of SHP's **Making of the UK** unit.
■ Pathway 3. In classes where SHP's *Societies in Change* or *Discovering The Making of the UK* is being used as the classroom textbook, the Picture Pack and the Teachers' Resource Book provide a wide range of materials to support slower learners and reluctant readers, by simplifying written source material and giving structure for pupils' written responses to questions in the textbook.

Main features of the support materials

These support materials respond to a number of the important requirements of low-attaining pupils:

Motivation
■ In common with the entire *Discovering the Past* series, the main aim of the support materials is to help pupils of all abilities to realise how fascinating history can be and to enjoy participating in history lessons.
■ The course is founded on the belief that pupils of all abilities can cope with investigation of real historical issues as long as they are presented at an appropriate level.
■ The materials aim to give pupils a high success rate – to increase motivation by ensuring positive achievement.

Differentiation
■ While the materials in SHP's **Making of the UK** unit are demonstrably capable of differentiation 'by outcome', there is often a need to differentiate 'by task'. Used alongside the core unit, these materials vastly increase the opportunities for differentiating pupils' work in Y8. The detailed teachers' notes which follow indicate many ways in which further differentiation can be achieved.

General learning skills
■ The materials encourage a variety of methods of learning.
■ They also aim to involve pupils in decisions about their learning, making them aware of the learning objectives and helping them to recognise what progress they are making.

Minimum entitlement
■ The authors have defined a minimum entitlement for **The Making of the UK** with four main focus points: 'Life in the 1500s', 'Religious changes in the 1500s', 'The Civil War', and 'Social changes 1500–1750'.

Language skills
■ The support materials have not been written to a single formula – nor have they been written at a single level. Instead, the language level of the authors' text, the written sources and the tasks has been carefully monitored to ensure it is totally suited to the nature of the material and the learning context of the pupils. For example, in certain tasks where group learning is being encouraged and pupils can gain support from their peers, a higher level of language is deemed appropriate than where pupils are working independently.
■ The materials are designed to complement the language policy of the school in a number of ways:

- by enhancing pupils' general reading skills
- by developing pupils' subject-specific vocabulary (through the use of a feature called 'History Dictionary')
- by developing higher-order reading skills, such as text interrogation and cross-referencing skills
- by ensuring that pupils' writing tasks are always undertaken for a purpose and for a good range of purposes
- by providing plentiful opportunities for group discussion.

Using these support materials

In this book you will find almost 200 photocopiable worksheets which cover key aspects of the programme of study for **The Making of the UK**, with a particular focus on:

■ society in the 1500s (Sections 2 and 3, Tasks 2–12)

■ religious change in the 1500s (Section 4, Tasks 13–22)

■ political changes in the 1600s (Sections 5–7, Tasks 23–27).

Planning your course

There are two main ways to use these materials.

1. They can be used as a self-standing course. We have covered the main areas of the programme of study for **The Making of the UK** and all the key elements of the unit. The activities are self-contained in that all the sources and resources you need to run the activities are provided for you in the Teachers' Resource Book and in the companion Picture Pack. There is no requirement that you have stocks of *Societies in Change*, *Discovering The Making of the UK* or any other textbook. These materials can provide you with a worksheet-based course which can be used alongside any textbook or none.

2. They can equally well be used to support the use of SHP's **Making of the UK** unit in schools which are already using *Societies in Change* or *Discovering The Making of the UK*. The aim has been to make selected enquiries more accessible to those with learning difficulties. This has been achieved by:

■ giving additional structure for pupils' tasks

■ narrowing the selection of source material for pupils to work with

■ further simplifying the language of the written sources

■ providing much bigger visuals for the pupils to work with (in the Picture Pack)

■ helping teachers to identify where pupils need help in making progress in history.

This book provides differentiated materials which enable pupils with learning difficulties to examine the same issues and tackle the same enquiries as mainstream pupils using *Societies in Change*. It allows them to develop their understanding of the same historical concepts as the rest of the class, but at their own pace and to their own level. And as their understanding grows, some pupils will be able to move confidently from support materials to textbook – choosing to work on the tasks in *Societies in Change* in preference to the tasks in this book.

Trialling experience has shown that in practice these materials are immensely flexible and that they can also provide invaluable support for pupils of a much wider range of abilities than simply those with learning difficulties. In some schools, tasks such as 23 and 24 on the Civil War have proved useful as a starting point for entire classes, leading them into the relevant enquiries in *Societies in Change*.

Differentiation

Differentiation is about helping pupils to progress at their own speed – hardly a novel idea. Yet the word sometimes fills people with fear, maybe because it has become the focus of recent criticism by OFSTED inspectors.

The problem is, of course, that all pupils are different, yet are usually taught together in groups of about thirty. How can teachers help each of them to progress at his/her own pace? These materials will offer you a practical set of strategies for achieving differentiation in your history teaching. However, some preliminary words of caution are needed. Discussion about differentiation is too often hampered by the assumption that it simply involves giving pupils different work to do. This obscures the fact that if pupils are to make progress then some more basic aspects of good practice are important. These following aspects of good practice have formed the bedrock of the strategies in the support materials:

1. Making aims and objectives clear We have tried to set clear aims and objectives and to help pupils understand what these are. The detailed notes which follow describe the aims of each task. We would encourage you always to talk with pupils about what is being done and why. This applies both on the overall level of planning a route through the unit (see page 8), and at the level of the individual exercise.

2. Making objectives achievable We have tried to ensure that these tasks can be tackled at a range of levels. Only you will know what is really achievable with your individual pupils – so we have tried to give you plenty of opportunities to set specific, itemised, achievable objectives for each pupil. (See also the notes on the Special Needs Code of Practice on page 5.)

A sample worksheet

Header shows the number of worksheet pages needed to do this task, and 'You will need' lists other materials pupils will require to complete the activity. These features help put pupils more effectively in control of their own learning.

History Dictionary box
Whenever necessary this book provides the support pupils need in order to understand subject-specific vocabulary *before* they meet the word in the worksheet. You can, if you wish, add other words to the History Dictionary box before you make photocopies.

Worksheet title

Introductory text
This is kept to the minimum necessary to introduce the task. Further background information and help with contextualising the task are provided in the detailed teachers' notes for you to use if you think it necessary.

'Your task'
• This is presented to a standard format.
• Stages in a task are numbered clearly.
• An adequate space is left for pupils to write or draw their own answers on this sheet if required.

Icons indicate the nature of the task.

reading

writing or drawing

cutting

sequencing or matching

discussion

game

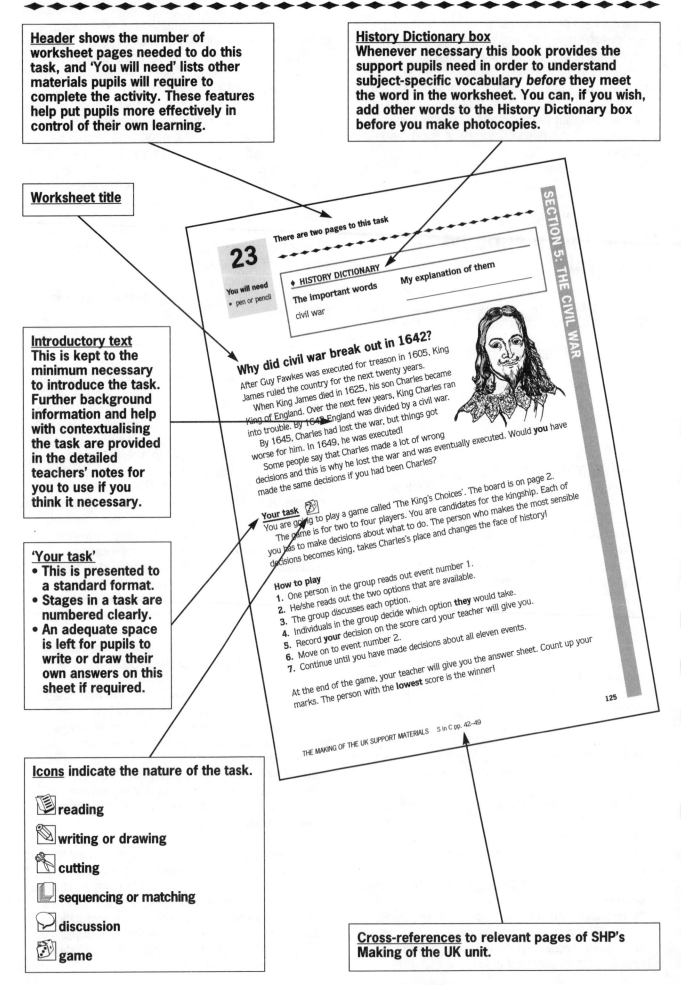

SECTION 5: THE CIVIL WAR

There are two pages to this task

23

You will need
• pen or pencil

◆ HISTORY DICTIONARY	
The important words	**My explanation of them**
civil war	

Why did civil war break out in 1642?
After Guy Fawkes was executed for treason in 1605, King James ruled the country for the next twenty years.
When King James died in 1625, his son Charles became King of England. Over the next few years, King Charles ran into trouble. By 1642, England was divided by a civil war.
By 1645, Charles had lost the war, but things got worse for him. In 1649, he was executed!
Some people say that Charles made a lot of wrong decisions and this is why he lost the war and was eventually executed. Would **you** have made the same decisions if you had been Charles?

Your task
You are going to play a game called 'The King's Choices'. The board is on page 2.
The game is for two to four players. You are candidates for the kingship. Each of you has to make decisions about what to do. The person who makes the most sensible decisions becomes king, takes Charles's place and changes the face of history!

How to play
1. One person in the group reads out event number 1.
2. He/she reads out the two options that are available.
3. The group discusses each option.
4. Individuals in the group decide which option **they** would take.
5. Record **your** decision on the score card your teacher will give you.
6. Move on to event number 2.
7. Continue until you have made decisions about all eleven events.

At the end of the game, your teacher will give you the answer sheet. Count up your marks. The person with the **lowest** score is the winner!

125

THE MAKING OF THE UK SUPPORT MATERIALS   S in C pp. 42–49

Cross-references to relevant pages of SHP's Making of the UK unit.

3. Monitoring and assessing the progress the pupils are making If pupils are to make progress, formative assessment is essential and these materials offer plentiful opportunity for you to make your own written, narrative comments on pupils' work. These comments should identify and praise achievement but also provide signposts for future work. Talking with pupils about their work and encouraging self-assessment – by allowing them to select pieces of their own work to display in a portfolio – is an effective way of encouraging progress.

4. Building on what the pupils already understand and re-applying skills and understanding in a new context In rough terms about 80 per cent of what takes place in a lesson should be consolidating what has already been achieved in terms of skills and understanding. About 20 per cent should involve setting pupils new challenges or introducing new ideas. If you go any faster you will risk losing many pupils; if you go more slowly, they may be bored through a lack of challenge. Throughout this material we have therefore introduced new content and ideas gradually, step-by-step, and offered regular opportunities for pupils to revisit skills and concepts in a new context.

5. Using a variety of teaching and learning styles Pupils are best motivated by the use of a range of learning situations and teaching methods. These materials can give them the experience of whole class work, small group work, work in pairs and individual work. There are opportunities for discussion as well as writing, drawing, matching, sequencing and source interrogation. One should not underestimate the power of the well-told story in history teaching. A story therefore forms the backbone of pupils' work on religious change in the 1500s.

6. Encouraging pupils to experiment and take risks We have avoided activities which deal mostly in 'right and wrong' answers. They lead to pupils becoming discouraged. They will avoid participating because of the fear of making mistakes. We have preferred to use open questions and problem-solving enquiries where all genuine efforts can be praised. By encouraging group work and allowing pupils to work in small groups with others of similar ability it should be possible, with careful planning, for each pupil to make a valuable contribution to the overall group effort.

The most essential factor in differentiation remains the role of the teacher in the classroom. Many teachers will offer appropriate support to pupils of different abilities as a matter of course. This can take various forms. It is worth your considering how effectively this is done in your own department.

Teachers will often rephrase explanations and instructions for the whole class. Extra explanation and support will be given to individual pupils as the teacher walks around the classroom discussing the work. During these discussions teachers might provide more structure for some pupils or reduce the demands by helping with the first few steps of the work. They might point individual pupils towards other resources which will help them with their work.

There will never be just one correct approach to differentiation, and effective differentiation cannot be achieved overnight. You will constantly need to adapt and adjust your teaching methods and your presentation of activities to allow individual pupils to progress. The bulk of the detailed notes on pages 13–20 is concerned with the matter of how to achieve further differentiation for individual pupils by varying the input and support given, by providing additional structure for an answer, and by asking pupils to respond in different ways.

The Code of Practice on Special Educational Needs

Working together to enable children with a range of needs to learn effectively has always been recognised as good educational practice. 'It presents teachers with some of the most challenging and rewarding work the education service can offer.' (Code of Practice on Special Educational Needs 1994)

Every school's special needs policy now reflects the 'Staged Response to Learning Needs' which was outlined in the 1994 Code of Practice, and all teachers are expected to demonstrate how they differentiate children's learning experiences to meet these needs. The **Making of the UK** support materials have been written to enable teachers to plan learning experiences which cover a wide range of learning needs and which can link both directly and indirectly with the core textbook.

Planning for Stage 1 of the 'Staged Response to Learning Needs'

There are several stages of learning need for which teachers now have to plan (see fig. 1 on page 6). Most children with special needs are within the first stage. Their understanding and enjoyment of history will grow through using the **Making of the UK** support materials as a stimulus for more in-depth work from a textbook (whichever this may be). They will also make progress as a result of the time teachers always invest in quality discussion and explanation with children who are learning more slowly.

When planning history for these children, teachers will be able to use their normal schemes of work, highlighting or underlining the planned activities and resources which have been differentiated for those children within Stage 1. The blank matrix on page 7 will be a useful tool in such planning. Teachers could also record in their class register which children fall into this category so that it is clear at whom the differentiated planning has been targeted.

Planning for Stages 2 and 3

For those children whose learning needs are more complex and who fall within Stages 2 and 3, planning, monitoring and evaluation intensify. The Special Needs Co-ordinator and possibly the Support Services will be involved. The **Making of the UK** materials have been designed to present achievable targets for these children too. The matrix on page 7 (see the Medieval Realms Support Materials Teachers' Resource Book for an example of its use) enables teachers to set targets for pupils who have been identified as having general learning difficulties. These targets would normally be agreed upon with the Special Needs Co-ordinator, the support teacher and, where appropriate, the child him/herself. The targets for Stages 2 and 3 are a focus of particular attention at OFSTED inspections.

Children's individual entitlement

We are all aware that learning does not always progress in a clear linear fashion, and children do not always remain conveniently within the stages provided by the Code of Practice! However, these support materials, in defining the minimum entitlement for each topic, and in providing differentiated tasks, provide a framework within which children can progress at a rate which suits their individual learning needs.

Stage 1: **Class or subject teachers** identify or register a child's special educational needs and, consulting the school's SEN Co-ordinator, take initial action.

Stage 2: The school's **SEN Co-ordinator** takes the lead responsibility for gathering information and for co-ordinating the child's special educational provision, working with the child's teachers.

Stage 3: Teachers and the SEN Co-ordinator are supported by **specialists from outside the school.**

Stage 4: **The LEA** considers the need for a statutory assessment and, if appropriate, makes a multidisciplinary assessment.

Stage 5: **The LEA** considers the need for a statement of special educational needs and, if appropriate, makes a statement and arranges, monitors and reviews provision.

Schools and LEAs will need to be able to demonstrate, in their arrangements for children with special educational needs, that they are fulfilling their statutory duty to have regard for this code. In the case of schools, OFSTED and OHMCI (Wales) inspection teams will consider the effectiveness of schools' policies and practices and the extent to which schools have had regard for the code.

Fig. 1 Stages of Provision

Practical considerations

Preparation

Many of the tasks do require a certain amount of preparation. We have attempted to highlight in the detailed notes where there is a particular need for this. However, here are a few general points to bear in mind.

For activities such as Tasks 1, 6 and 29 you can enlarge pictures, captions and text before cutting them out. Mounting these on thin card and laminating them extends their shelf life and means less preparation the following year!

There are some 'resource sheets' – e.g. question cards for Task 6 – which need copying on to card of different colours.

Most of the tasks have more than one page. You can give the sheets out one by one. Occasionally the later sheets in the task are 'extension sheets' only, to be available if a pupil asks for them.

If you are planning to use the 'History Dictionary' feature, you will need to photocopy the definitions on pages 193–198 on to card.

The teaching environment

Don't forget how much the teaching environment can help pupils. The walls of the classroom are a potential resource if you cover them with helpful illustrations, charts, diagrams and timelines to which pupils can refer.

Reference material (e.g. the History Dictionary file – see below) should be readily available.

A pupil folder

There are obvious benefits in pupils creating a **Making of the UK** folder in which to store their completed drawings, written answers, worksheets, and their larger pieces of work.

To give extra coherence and status to this file, there is a photocopiable 'title page' for pupils to personalise for the front of their folders (see page 10). In the centre pupils should stick in or draw a picture which they feel expresses something important about the period. It is worth spending time over this and perhaps turning it into a discussion activity in which pupils compare and talk about the pictures they have chosen.

There are also two photocopiable templates (lined for written work and unlined for artwork), both with attractive borders and spaces for pupils to write in their names, the date and the topic. Hopefully these will encourage pupils to take a pride in their work. You will find these templates on pages 11 and 12 of this book.

Teachers could encourage pupils to think in terms of constructing their own history book.

The rationale behind pupils using their own workbook together with the Picture Pack is similarly for them to feel that their work has status and permanence.

Year 8 History Unit:

Names of Pupils

....

....

General target

Support planned

Specific target for this lesson

content	vocabulary	key questions	historical skills and concepts	teaching and learning activity	resources

My pathway through The Making of the UK

Name _____

Term _____

Subjects to be investigated	Date completed
Subject: _____	_____
1. _____	_____
2. _____	_____
3. _____	_____
Subject: _____	_____
1. _____	_____
2. _____	_____
3. _____	_____
Subject: _____	_____
1. _____	_____
2. _____	_____
3. _____	_____

'My route through *The Making of the UK*'

An important part of ensuring motivation is setting appropriate achievable targets and allowing pupils to monitor their own progress against these targets (see above under 'Differentiation'). The photocopiable planning sheet on page 12 is designed to help teacher and pupil plan together and record progress. Pupils should fill in this chart in discussion with their teacher. They can then decorate it and add it to their folder. It should also be copied for your own records. Use and adapt the sheet however you wish, but we envisage that the three subject headings will reflect the three main areas of the course – society in the 1500s, religious change in the 1500s and political change in the 1600s – and that the numbered lines will list the most important tasks pupils are going to tackle.

Timelines

All pupils need a chronological framework, not just those with learning difficulties. It would be useful to have the following two timelines prepared:

1. A horizontal timeline spanning around 5000 years, with the names of different eras, and in relevant sections dating by centuries. You could use frieze paper or wallpaper for this. You should already have this if you have used the Medieval Realms support materials.

Whenever pupils are being introduced to a new study unit or are revising their skills of chronology, they should look at this timeline. It is important that they are helped gradually to develop an understanding of where, in general terms, **The Making of the UK** stands in relation to, e.g., **Medieval Realms** or even, from KS2, **The Tudors**.

2. The other timeline should be for the period the class is studying; in this case 1500–1750. This should be on as large a scale as possible – dating by decades is ideal. The timeline could be mounted on sugar paper or wallpaper lining and pinned to the wall.

As well as dates, give it shape by adding kings/queens and pictures of the main events (as in Task 1).

Pupils can add to the timeline as their knowledge and understanding of the period increase.

Sometimes it is useful to divide the timeline up into parallel sections – one row each for political, social, economic and cultural developments. Each section can be colour-coded and added to as and when the need arises.

The History Dictionary

Throughout their study of history, pupils will come across strange and unfamiliar vocabulary. One recommendation of this course is that pupils compile their own history dictionary. They could do the same for each study unit.

This dictionary can be either a small (indexed) book – such as you can buy very cheaply in a stationer's – or it can be a set of sheets in the back of pupils' **Making of the UK** folders.

Each time pupils come across an unknown or important new word, they should be encouraged to record it in their own dictionary – and they can also illustrate it if they wish.

Throughout the tasks in this book, new words are introduced and explained. The key ones are included in a History Dictionary box at the head of the worksheet. A definition can be given by the teacher or worked out by the pupil. Teachers should remind pupils to transfer these words and concepts into their own 'History Dictionaries'. Wherever possible we have deliberately tried to leave space in the History Dictionary box so that you can add other words which you think your pupils will have trouble with before you copy the worksheet.

To help pupils who wish to write their own definitions, we have provided a photocopiable set of definitions of the key terms (pages 193–198). These can be photocopied on to card and kept available in a file in the classroom for pupils to consult when they are writing their definitions.

The dictionary definitions can also be used in other ways. For example, you can give pupils two or three definitions and ask them to find pictorial sources in the textbook or in the Picture Pack to illustrate them.

The Picture Pack

The Picture Pack forms an essential part of this bank of resources. It contains 18 full-colour, laminated images at large size, some chosen from *Societies in Change*, and others entirely new pictures which extend the range of visual sources and can be used for comparative work.

Experience has shown that some pupils find it easier still to work with black and white outline drawings of these sources – because these can simplify some of the detail of the original image, and be used for pupils to label and mark. Outlines of all 18 images can be found on pages 199–214 of this book.

THE MAKING OF THE UK

Name _____   Class _____

Year _____   School _____

Name _____

Date _____

Topic _____

Name _____

Date _____

Topic _____

_____

_____

_____

_____

_____

_____

_____

_____

_____

_____

_____

_____

_____

_____

Teachers' notes

The aims of the detailed notes which follow are:
- to summarise the aims of each activity
- to highlight any preparation that may be necessary
- to suggest how to use the activities to maximum effect in the classroom, and in particular to indicate links with SHP's **Making of the UK** unit
- to suggest how further differentiation can be achieved by adjusting the way in which the task is presented. Some of the suggestions for differentiation will, we hope, stretch the more able, whilst others will allow still greater access for the least able.

To indicate which way the extension lies, we have used symbols as follows:

[↗] upward extension which makes the task more challenging for pupils who are improving more rapidly

[↔] an alternative approach to the activity which we think is neither easier nor more difficult than the task we have set, but simply allows for a variety of teaching styles

[↙] downward extension which makes the task more accessible still

Section 1: Overview

The first two tasks a) introduce pupils to the kings, queens and main events of the period, establishing the background for their subsequent work on political and religious change; and b) set the context for the tasks in which they find out about the lives of ordinary people in the sixteenth century.

Task 1: Getting to know the period

Aim: for pupils to identify some of the key events and personalities that they will encounter in their study of The Making of the UK.

Preparation: You could enlarge the resource sheets to A3 size. Enlarging them on to card will increase their durability.

Your task: This exercise consciously builds on and progresses from the timeline activities at the beginning of the Medieval Realms materials.
   The completed timeline can either be glued on to an A3 sheet of paper, or if pupils are using cards, once they have completed the timeline accurately, they could colour the pictures so that they look more interesting and attractive for subsequent users! In this case, give pupils a photocopy of Resource Sheet 3 to glue inside their books or keep in their folders.

[↔] Discuss in class what pupils already know about any of the events mentioned.

[↗] Each class member takes one event or monarch. He/she researches into that particular

event/monarch and produces half a page of information to give more detail to the timeline.

[↔] Pupils play the following game in twos or threes. They take the picture and description cards only, and place them face down on the table. They play 'Threes' (i.e. the same game as 'Pairs'). The winner is the one with the most 'threes'.

[↙] Depending on the needs of individual pupils, you can give them a partly completed timeline, so they only have to match up the bottom set of picture cards, for example, or put half of the monarchs into order.

[↗] By cutting along every line of the full version on Resource Sheet 3, an entire jigsaw can be created for individuals or groups to complete.

Task 2: England in the 1500s

(*S in C* pp.2–5)

Aim: for pupils to develop an awareness of what were the main physical features of England in the 1500s and how they were different from nowadays

Your task:

[↗] Pupils add two or three further sentences to the descriptions of England in the 1500s.

(page 6)
Your task:

[↙] Pupils list things which would not have been there in 1500 without necessarily giving reasons.

[↙] Pupils select only one or two pictures to examine.

(page 7)
Your task:

[↙] Pupils add speech and thought bubbles to the picture instead of writing their ideas on page 7.

Section 2: The poor and the rich

After a general survey of the different social groups of the time, pupils go on to consider how beggars were looked upon and treated, and then tackle the whole issue of poverty in the sixteenth century and its causes. The section ends with a game to reinforce their understanding of this topic.

Task 3: What sorts of people lived in England in the 1500s?

(*S in C* p.3, Picture Sources 2, 4, 15)

Aim: for pupils to gain an understanding of the different levels of society which existed in sixteenth- and seventeenth-century England

Your task:

[↙] Pupils could first be given just two sets to match, e.g. the gentleman and the labourer. They then attempt the other two categories.

↗ Pupils use information from the relevant pictorial sources on pages 7–15 of *Societies in Change* to add a description of the interior of each house.

↔ You could select pictures from the Picture Pack, e.g. 2, 4 and 15, and ask pupils to look for examples of gentlemen, citizens, etc.

Task 4: Were the poor really poor?

(*S in C* pp. 6–11, Picture Source 1)

Aim: to further develop pupils' knowledge and understanding of the different social groups in England

(page 4)
Your task: The pictures and descriptions should be matched as follows: A The Abraham Man, B The Upright Man, C The Counterfeit Crank, D The Clapper Dudgeon, E Bawdy Baskets, F The Doxy.

↙ The relevant text for each beggar is in bold in the descriptions on page 5. This could be extracted and written on flashcards. Pupils glue the text underneath the correct picture.

↙ Two descriptions, e.g. the Clapper Dudgeon and the Upright Man, can be matched in advance so that pupils only have to match the remaining pictures and descriptions.

↗ Pupils do the activity on page 7 of *Societies in Change*.

(page 6)
Your task:
↔ Pupils underline the key phrases or sentences which they used to make their deductions.

↗ Pupils do question 1 at the bottom of page 7 of *Societies in Change* which requires them to compare Sources 3 and 4.

↔ Use Picture Source 1 to reinforce pupils' understanding of what contemporaries saw as the three different types of beggars.

Task 5: Why were people poor?

(*S in C* p.8)

Aim: for pupils to understand that there are many reasons why there was such great poverty in England at this time

Your task:
↙ Pupils can use Resource Sheet 1 only, which includes the more concrete and straightforward causes and consequences.

Task 6: Poverty Pursuits

Aim: to reinforce pupils' understanding of the causes and consequences of poverty which were introduced in Task 5

Preparation: You could enlarge the board to A3 size or on to card. The resource sheets need copying on to coloured card and cutting into a pack of cards.

Your task:
↗ Pupils could be given only half the question cards and asked to write nine more questions of their own based on the information in Task 5.

↗ Pupils could be given cards without answers and, in teams, have to find out the answers from Task 5.

Section 3: Private lives

Pupils investigate aspects of marriage and family life in the sixteenth and seventeenth centuries, discovering both the usefulness and the limitations of evidence from the period. The section ends with a task encouraging pupils to compare forms of entertainment in this period with those of the present day.

Task 7: Finding out about private lives

(*S in C* p.16)

Aim: for pupils to see how the availability of evidence affects what we study in history

Your task:
↙ The questions could be used as the basis for a class discussion, in which case there is no need for pupils to write or record anything since teachers collate all the necessary information on the blackboard.

Task 8: Getting married

(*S in C* pp.16–17, Picture Source 4)

Aim: for pupils to test the viewpoint of a modern historian against evidence from the sixteenth and seventeenth centuries

Your task:
↙ Pupils could be given only two or three of the sources on page 2.

↗ The teacher whites out the written sources so that pupils only have the timeline dates and names. They look for the correct sources from pages 16 and 17 of *Societies in Change*. Then they write them in the blank squares.

↔ Question 4 is used as a discussion question only.

(page 3)
Your task:
↔ Pupils underline the sentences and phrases in the Duke of Richmond's letter which indicate he was only interested in making money, not in the well-being of his son.

(page 4)
Your task:
↙ Before attempting the activity, have a class discussion about the merits and demerits of arranged marriages in a seventeenth-century context. This will produce more profound insights in the pupils' letters.

→ Pupils could alternatively choose to write about the wedding shown in Picture Source 4.

Task 9: Being married

(*S in C* pp.18–19)

Aim: to look at sixteenth- and seventeenth-century marriage from a male point of view

Your task:

↔ Pupils rewrite the bishop's speech in Source 1 using modern-day idiom (no swear words!).

Task 10: Being married – a woman's viewpoint

(*S in C* pp.18–19)

Aim: to look at sixteenth- and seventeenth-century marriage from a woman's point of view

Your task:

↔ Pupils read, or have read to them, Pepys' diary. They discuss in small groups what they think about his attitude towards his wife. They then report their conclusions to the rest of the class.

↙ You could write in partially completed entries for Elizabeth Pepys' diary before photocopying the sheet.

↙ Pupils are given the line drawing of Pepys and his wife (page 1). Round its edge, they put in other word bubbles which show the couple's attitudes towards each other, based on the evidence of Pepys' diary.

↙ Pupils choose only one date in Pepys' diary to annotate.

↗ Pupils answer questions 6, 7 and 8 on page 19 of *Societies in Change*.

↔ If pupils tackled the 'wife sale' activity in Task 9, they could now make a similar poster for a 'husband sale'.

Task 11: Having children

(*S in C* pp.19–21)

Aim: for pupils to appreciate the reasons for and feelings about infant mortality in this period

Preparation: Photocopy the Happy Family descriptions (pages 67–70) on to coloured card and cut them up into a pack of cards.

Your task: As always, use this game sensitively – be aware that some children may have recent experience of tragedy in their own families.

↔ Pupils play the game and then use it as a basis for a whole class discussion centred on the likely reasons for such high infant mortality.

(page 3)
Your task: The original of this picture is on page 21 of *Societies in Change*.

↗ Pupils do the activities on page 21 of *Societies in Change*.

Task 12: Could you enjoy yourself in the sixteenth and seventeenth centuries?

(*S in C* pp.22–23, Picture Source 3)

Aim: to see the range of sports and activities enjoyed by rich and poor

Your task: We cannot think of a sport for the letters X and Z. If you do, please tell us! If you have difficulties with E, how about equestrianism?

(page 2)
Your task:

✓ The task can be simplified by completing some more of the labelling before pupils are given the worksheet.

✓ Pupils could work in pairs, one of them doing the task on page 2 and the other that on page 3. They compare notes before attempting page 5 together.

(page 6)
Your task:

✓ Pupils discuss questions 2–4 rather than writing the answers down.

↗ Pupils answer questions 2, 3 and 6 on page 23 of *Societies in Change*.

Section 4: Religious changes in the 1500s

The activities in this section are structured to build one from the other, giving a step-by-step understanding of the religious changes of the period. The centre piece of the section is a story to reinforce pupils' knowledge and involve them in the lives of ordinary people who lived through these changes.

Task 13: What religion did people follow in 1500?

(*S in C* pp.26–27)

Aim: for pupils to understand the key features of religion in England in 1500. This forms the basis for looking at change in the sixteenth century

(page 2)
Your task:

✓ Pupils could cut out the drawings on pages 1 and 2 and stick them onto Richard Berne's tomb (page 3).

(pages 4 and 5)
Your task:

✓ Question 2 on page 4 could be used for class discussion rather than written work, as could question 2 on page 5.

Task 14: Who were the Protestants?

(*S in C* pp.28–31)

Aim: This is an information sheet which lays out the essential protests or criticisms made by the Protestants, as a prelude to Task 15

Task 15: What is King Henry VIII famous for?

(*S in C* pp.28–29, Picture Source 7)

Aim: to explore the reasons why Henry VIII quarrelled with the Pope

(page 3)

Your task: There is a lot of information on pages 1 and 2 and the purpose of the task is to encourage pupils to process it.

✔ You could write some example questions and answers before you copy this sheet.

↔ Pupils could tackle the activity on Picture Source 7 in the Picture Pack, which also goes into the reasons for Henry's break with the Pope.

Task 16: What is Queen Mary famous for?

(*S in C* pp.32–33)

Aim: for pupils to see how strongly people felt about religion and religious changes in this period

(page 3)

Your task:

↔ You could start with the rhyme activity, before going back to the tasks on pages 1 and 2.

Task 17: What changes did the Tudor kings and queens make?

Aim: to summarise the religious 'to-ing and fro-ing' of the Tudor monarchs through the sixteenth century

Task 18: How did changes in religion affect ordinary people?

(*S in C* pp.34–35)

Aim: to summarise the impact of the changes in religious policy on ordinary people in ordinary churches

Your task:

↙ This recaps on Task 13 to reinforce understanding of Protestant attitudes and habits. If it is appropriate for your class, you could go straight on to the task on page 2, which deals with the more concrete changes.

(pages 3 and 4)

These are outline drawings of colour pictures you will find on pages 26 and 31 of *Societies in Change*.

Your task:

↙ The pictures can be used as the basis for class discussion rather than written work.

↗ Pupils could be given just the pictures and asked to write a description of each church, identifying which is the Catholic and which the Protestant.

Task 19: A Family Affair

(*S in C* pp.34–35)

Aims: to reinforce pupils' understanding of religious changes in this period; and for pupils to realise what impact the Reformation had on ordinary people

Your task: A variety of strategies for telling and using stories such as this were described in the Medieval Realms support materials. For example, you can:

a) read the story yourself, then give pupils the illustrations only, which they have to sequence from their memory of the story.

b) give pupils the story but with the picture captions whited out. Their first task is to write the captions.

c) ask pupils to choose one other moment in the story to illustrate.

d) tape the story so that pupils can listen to it again and again.

e) follow the story with a class discussion. What were the main events of the story? Would they have helped their relatives in similar circumstances?

↔ Using the first two pictures and captions as a starting point, lead a class discussion around the following questions: Great-Uncle John told Emma and Ben about the old days; what do you know about life in Tudor England before 1600? Can you remember why King Henry wanted a divorce? What were the main differences between Catholic and Protestant ways?

(page 1)
Your task:

↙ The teacher completes the timeline him/herself and cuts it into strips. Pupils sequence the timeline and glue it onto an A4 sheet.

↗ Pupils find the dates as well as the events for themselves.

(page 8)
Your task:

↔ Pupils do this activity after discussing with the teacher what each person might have thought.

✔ Pupils choose two people only.

(page 9)
Your task: There are many possible ways of developing work on this story and these characters.

↔ Pupils could think of a different ending to the story. They read their endings out. The class decides which is their favourite 'new ending'. Could it have happened?

↔ Pupils could write the next chapter of the story, explaining what they think happened to Ben and Emma. The class decides which is the most likely scenario.

Task 20: Who were the Puritans?

(*S in C* pp.24–25, Picture Sources 4 and 6b)

Aim: to give pupils some idea of what the Puritans believed in

Your task:

↗ Pupils write their own captions for the pictures.

↔ Pupils describe what they do on Sundays. Class discussion: Which of their actions would the Puritans have approved of and which would they have disapproved of?

↔ Pupils also look at Picture Sources 4 and 6b. What makes us think that some of the people in these pictures are Puritans?

(page 6)

Preparation: Enlarge the board to A3 and copy it, once per pupil.

↗ In preparation for this activity, pupils go through the sources on page 25 of *Societies in Change* with the teacher. He/she records on the board all the 'good' and 'bad' things that are found. Pupils put them in rank order. This will help them to decide how long the snakes and ladders need to be!

Task 21: Why did England become a Protestant country?

Aim: to review the causes of the English Reformation

Your task:

↙ Each reason could be written on a separate piece of paper and pupils are given only two or four to choose from.

Task 22: Were the Catholics framed?

(*S in C* pp.36–39)

Aims: to remind pupils who the main monarchs were during this period, and for pupils to investigate sources of evidence about the Gunpowder Plot and to draw their own conclusions

Your task:

↗ Pupils have a blank family tree which they complete themselves.

(page 5)

Your task:

↙ Pupils work in groups. They come to a decision about each question. The best 'writer' records the answers for the whole group. Each pupil could then fill in their own report form (page 8).

↗ Pupils do the activity on page 39 of *Societies in Change*.

Section 5: The Civil War

This section includes an investigation of the causes of the Civil War (by means of a game in which pupils consider each step towards the war from the King's point of view) and the reality of the war for different people of the period.

Task 23: Why did civil war break out in 1642?

(*S in C* pp.42–49)

Aim: for pupils to understand the main causes of the Civil War

Your task:

↗ A good extension activity would be to ask pupils to make a list of all the causes of the Civil War under the headings 'social', 'political', 'religious' and 'economic'.

↗ Pupils take each of the causes outlined in the game and read pages 42–49 of *Societies in Change* to find out about them in more detail.

↗ Pupils read pages 42–49 of *Societies in Change* and make a list of any further causes of the English Civil War that they can find.

Task 24: What was life like during the Civil War?

(*S in C* pp.52–55)

Aim: for pupils to empathise with people whose lives were affected by the war

Your task:

↔ Pupils can gain additional information for their poster from pages 54 and 55 of *Societies in Change*.

↗ Pupils answer question 3 on page 55 of *Societies in Change*.

(page 2)

Your task:

↙ The teacher gives pupils either the letters written by Lady Harley or those written by William Vavasour to sort chronologically. Only after this has been done do they put them together.

↔ Rather than write an account of the siege, pupils create a broadsheet with eight or nine drawings and captions describing the siege. They choose to write the broadsheet either as a Parliamentarian or as a Royalist.

↗ Pupils answer questions 1–4 on page 54 of *Societies in Change*.

Section 6: The execution of Charles I

Pupils are encouraged to consider the issues behind the event of the execution, as well as use contemporary evidence to find out about the trial and perhaps re-enact it.

Task 25: Why did the English execute their king?

(*S in C* pp.58–59)

Tasks 25 and 26 belong together.
Aim: for pupils to understand what a significant event in English history the trial and execution of Charles I was

Your task:

✓ You could fill in more boxes for the pupils before copying the sheet.

Task 26: The Trial of King Charles I – a play

(*S in C* pp.58–61, Picture Source 12)

↗ Pupils look for the source references on pages 58–60 of *Societies in Change* and identify those which were used to help write the play.

↗ The teacher blanks out King Charles's lines. Pupils read through the text on pages 58–60 of *Societies in Change* in order to write in Charles's lines themselves.

↗ Pupils write all of Act Two themselves, using Picture Source 12 to help them.

↗ Pupils are given the beginning and end of the play. They write the middle section themselves.

↗ Pupils do question 2 on page 60 of *Societies in Change*.

Section 7: Cromwell

Pupils use evidence from the period to find out about Oliver Cromwell. As always, the flexibility of the task means that this difficult topic can be adapted for pupils of varying abilities.

Task 27: What kind of man was Oliver Cromwell?

(*S in C* pp.64–67)

Aim: for pupils to investigate reasons why Oliver Cromwell acted as he did

Your task:

✓ The teacher constructs a date timeline so that pupils only have to add the correct information for each date.

(page 3)
Your task: This is a difficult exercise which teachers may feel needs to be done as a whole class discussion so that they can explain the nature, context and language of the written sources.

Section 8: The Great Plague and the Fire of London

The activities in this section build on what pupils learnt about the Black Death in Medieval Realms, encouraging them to consider the plague objectively through various contemporary sources and also to put themselves in the shoes of people of the time in a role play. They go on to consider the usefulness of various types of evidence in finding out about the Great Fire of London and to understand the importance of some of the changes which took place in London in the seventeenth century.

Task 28: How did the Great Plague affect the City of London?

(*S in C* pp.82–84)

Aim: for pupils to understand that people were no nearer finding the causes of plague and disease in the seventeenth century than they had been in the fourteenth century

Introduction: Discuss with pupils what they remember about the plague, its causes and effects, from their study of Medieval Realms.

Your task: The definitions of the causes of death can be found on page 34 of *Societies in Change* Teachers' Resource Book.

✓ Questions 1–3 can be tackled through discussion.

✓ Pupils could choose a particularly nasty-sounding disease, such as 'spotted fever and purples'. They design a poster which will go up in the street to warn people about the disease.

(page 4)
Your task:

✓ You can underline the ways in which people tried to avoid plague before copying the sheet. Pupils then have to write these ways in their own words.

↗ Question 5 is quite difficult. Pupils could discuss their ideas in class first of all.

Task 29: How do we know about the Great Plague?

(*S in C* p.84)

Aim: for pupils to investigate primary sources of evidence about the plague

Your task:

☑ The teacher matches the first, third, fifth, seventh and ninth pictures with their descriptions so that the task is more manageable.

☑ Pupils work in pairs. One has all the pictures, the other (the better reader) has all the text. Pupil 1 describes what he/she sees. His/her partner looks for the correct caption.

(page 6)

Your task:

☑ Questions 1–4 could be tackled through discussion.

Task 30: Plague comes to Eyam – September 1665

Aim: to develop pupils' knowledge and understanding of how the plague affected people's attitudes

Your task: Children should gather round in a large circle. Those who want Fullerton to come to the village sit on one side of the circle. Those who don't want him to come to the village sit on the other side.

What decision will they come to? The class teacher, in the guise of Sir George Saville's secretary, chairs the discussion and all the participants are allowed to speak. The chairperson has to make the final decision. Perhaps he/she will need a scribe to record the arguments? A pupil who has been absent could take this role, being a junior clerk in Sir George's employ.

Each character has been given a small pen portrait of him/herself, plus some ideas as to what he/she might say.

The children should also add other arguments they themselves have worked out. They should use contemporary evidence and could perhaps compose arguments about how they might prevent the plague and what cures they might use.

These character synopses should be given to the children well before the time when the debate will take place. Make sure that they don't see each other's pieces of paper!

The class teacher guides the discussion and, when he/she thinks it is flagging or perhaps getting out of hand, adds further arguments to fuel the debate.

↔ This is an ambitious role play that could be difficult to manage with a large, possibly boisterous class. Teachers might prefer to split the class into groups of four. Each member of the group is still given an individual role to research and provide an argument for. Two are 'for' and two are 'against' Fullerton coming. As they discuss and argue their cases, the teacher circulates and helps them to formulate worthwhile arguments. This is followed by whole class feedback, when either the opposing pairs or the pairs themselves report back on each other's points of view.

The plague did come to Eyam – but in George Vicars' cloth rather than via Matthew Fullerton! The village then performed an act of great self-sacrifice.

Under the influence of Mompesson, they voluntarily quarantined themselves off – no one was allowed to come or leave. More than half the villagers died, but the plague did not spread beyond Eyam. This could be the basis for a second stage of the role play, with the same characters discussing whether they should cut themselves off.

Task 31: How did London change?

(*S in C* pp.85–86)

Aim: for pupils to assess the impact that the Great Fire had on London's architecture

Your task:

☑ Arrows could be placed on the first picture, pointing to the danger spots. Pupils select from a list of these dangers, written out underneath.

☑ Questions 3 and 4 could be dealt with through discussion only.

Task 32: The story of the Great Fire of London

(*S in C* p.85, Picture Source 13a)

Aim: for pupils to see how evidence from the time can be used to reconstruct the story of the Fire

Your task:

↗ You could give only the first two parts of Hannah's story. White out Hannah's version of Sources 3, 4, 6 and 9. Pupils reconstruct the rest of her story from Sources 3–9.

↗ Pupils search for details in the sources which are not in Hannah's story and add speech bubbles.

Task 33: The London coffee houses

(*S in C* pp.86–87)

Aim: for pupils to understand some of the other social and economic changes which took place in London in the century after the Great Fire

Your task: There is a full-colour version of the coffee house picture on page 87 of *Societies in Change*.

Section 9: Uniting the kingdom

The final tasks summarise the events which led to the 'making of the United Kingdom'.

Task 34: Uniting the kingdom

(*S in C* pp.72–73)

Tasks 34 and 35 go together.

Aim: for pupils to understand how the political map of the British Isles changed in 250 years

Your task:

☑ The teacher omits question 4 from the worksheet.

Task 35: Which country?

Your task:

☑ The teacher can give pupils cards relating to only one of the countries. They put these into chronological order.

1

Getting to know the period

In this course you will be studying the sixteenth and seventeenth centuries. This was a time of great change in England. There was a civil war and a revolution and there were important changes in religion.

In this task you will get an overview of the period you will be studying. Your teacher will give you two sets of cards. The first shows the kings and queens who ruled England during this period. The second has descriptions and pictures of some of the events that took place.

For these tasks you will need to work on a large desk or table, and it is probably best to work with a partner.

Your task A

1. Your teacher will give you a set of cards with pictures of Tudor and Stuart kings and queens.
2. Put the kings and queens in the correct chronological order.
3. Between 1509 and 1603 the Tudor family ruled. The Stuarts ruled from 1603 to 1714. Put the period names in the correct places under the row of monarchs.

Your task B

1. Your teacher will give you some pictures and description cards. Match two pictures to each description.
2. Put the descriptions in chronological order.
3. Now put the events in the correct places – under the right monarchs.

You now have a choice. You can use these pictures and descriptions to make one large class timeline of the period, or you can ask your teacher for a copy of the completed timeline.

THE TUDORS

THE STUARTS

Henry VIII
1509–1547

Edward VI
1547–1553

Mary I
1553–1558

Elizabeth I
1558–1603

Anne
1702–1714

James I
1603–1625

Charles I
1625–1649

James II
1685–1688

Oliver Cromwell, and then his son, ruled instead of a king 1653–1659

Charles II
1660–1685

William and Mary of Orange
1689–1702

1530s
King Henry had six wives. He also made himself head of the Church of England.

1540s and 1550s
After Henry died, Edward became king. He was Protestant. The next monarch, Mary, was Catholic. The next queen, Elizabeth, kept some parts of the Catholic religion, but made the Church Protestant again.

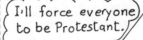

1580s
Elizabeth had problems with Mary Queen of Scots, who was Catholic. She had Mary executed. She also fought the Spanish Armada (fleet). The Spanish were Catholics. Elizabeth won.

1605
During King James's reign, some Catholics tried to blow up Parliament. Everyone remembers Guy Fawkes, who was one of the plotters. There were strict laws against the Catholics.

1640s

In 1642, King Charles and his Royalist army went to war against the Parliamentarian army. This civil war lasted until 1646. Eventually Parliament won and King Charles was beheaded in 1649.

1650s

A man called Oliver Cromwell, who had led the Parliamentarians, became leader of the country. After a while, people wanted a king again, so Charles's eldest son became Charles II in 1660.

1660s

In 1665, the plague came to England again. Half of the people in London died.
The plague only stopped in 1666 when a fire which started in a bakery burned most of London down.

SCOTLAND

IRELAND

WALES

LONDON

ENGLAND

ENGLAND · WALES · SCOTLAND IRELAND. All four nations were governed (ruled) from LONDON

And afterwards?

King James II was Catholic. He was replaced in 1688 by his sister Mary and her husband William of Orange, who became William III. They were both Protestants. By 1750, most of Britain was united under the English king.

THE TUDORS

| Henry VIII 1509–1547 | Edward VI 1547–1553 | Mary I 1553–1558 | Elizabeth I 1558–1603 |

THE STUARTS

| James I 1603–1625 | Charles I 1625–1649 | Oliver Cromwell, and then his son, ruled instead of a king 1653–1659 | Charles II 1660–1685 | James II 1685–1688 | William and Mary of Orange 1689–1702 | Anne 1702–1714 |

1530s
King Henry had six wives. He also made himself head of the Church of England.

1540s and 1550s
After Henry died, Edward became king. He was Protestant. The next monarch, Mary, was Catholic. The next queen, Elizabeth, kept some parts of the Catholic religion, but made the Church Protestant again.

1580s
Elizabeth had problems with Mary Queen of Scots, who was Catholic. She had Mary executed. She also fought the Spanish Armada (fleet). The Spanish were Catholics. Elizabeth won.

1605
During King James's reign, some Catholics tried to blow up Parliament. Everyone remembers Guy Fawkes, who was one of the plotters. There were strict laws against the Catholics.

1640s
In 1642, King Charles and his Royalist army went to war against the Parliamentarian army. This civil war lasted until 1646. Eventually Parliament won and King Charles was beheaded in 1649.

1650s
A man called Oliver Cromwell, who had led the Parliamentarians, became leader of the country. After a while, people wanted a king again, so Charles's eldest son became Charles II in 1660.

1660s
In 1665, the plague came to England again. Half of the people in London died. The plague only stopped in 1666 when a fire which started in a bakery burned most of London down.

And afterwards?
King James II was Catholic. He was replaced in 1688 by his sister Mary and her husband William of Orange, who became William III. They were both Protestants. By 1750, most of Britain was united under the English king.

ENGLAND • WALES • SCOTLAND • IRELAND. All four nations were governed (ruled) from LONDON

2

England in the 1500s

You will need

- pen or pencil
- scissors
- glue

How different was it from England today?

Five hundred years ago in 1500, England looked very different from how it looks today.

a There were huge forests where wild animals lived.

b Most of the farmers looked after sheep. Only a few of them grew crops.

c People grew their own food and looked after a few of their own animals.

d Most towns were really small and there were only a few big cities.

Your task

1. Examine the pictures on the next four pages carefully.
2. Complete the captions by putting in the correct date:1500s or 1990s.
3. Decide which description (from sentences **a** to **d** above) fits each picture of the 1500s. Write the descriptions in the boxes under the pictures.
4. Write your own descriptions for the pictures of the 1990s.
   Here is an example:

England in the _1990s_

People go shopping at
supermarkets...
_____
_____

England in the _1500s_

People grew their own food
and looked after a few of
their own animals
_____

2

England in the _____

England in the _____

England in the _____

England in the _____

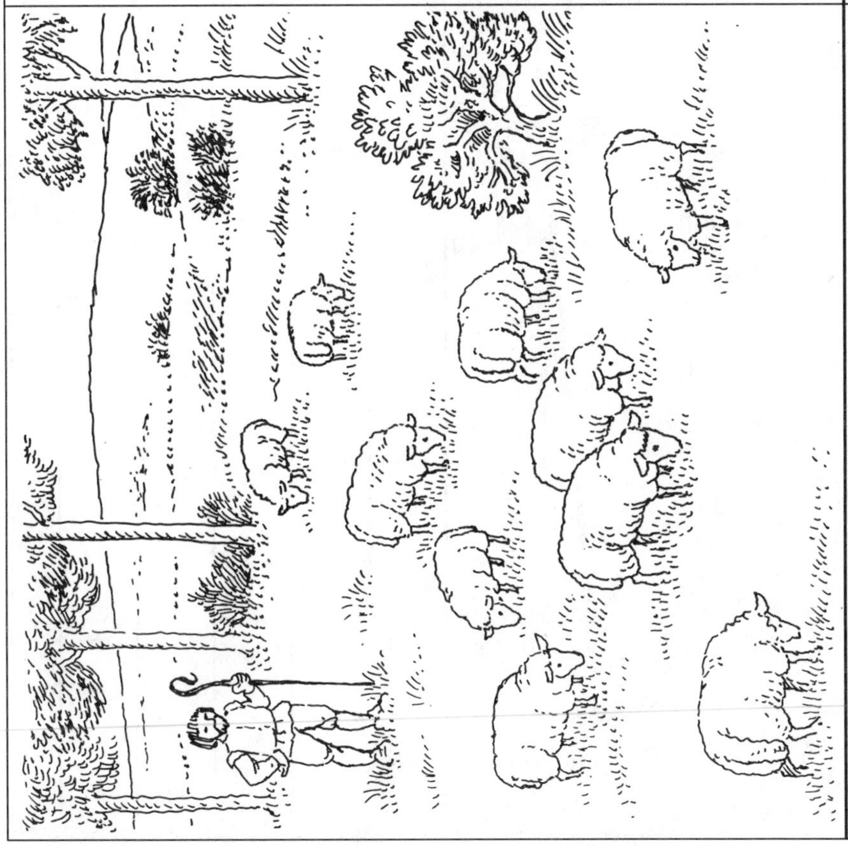

England in the _____

England in the _____

2

England in the _____

England in the _____

THE MAKING OF THE UK SUPPORT MATERIALS

◆–◆

Your task 🔍 ✏️
Take each modern-day picture in turn.
1. List all the things in the picture which you think would **not** have been there in 1500.
2. Write down next to each item on your list **why** it would not have been there.

For example:

Picture : The New Forest

Things which would not have been there in 1500	Reasons why they would not have been there
1. A modern estate car 2. Signposts and picnic places	Cars weren't invented in the 1500s. In those days, forests were very dangerous places because there were wild bears and wolves in them. People didn't visit them for day trips, so there was no need for signposts and picnic places!

Picture _____

Things which would not have been there in 1500	Reasons why they would not have been there

◆◆◆◆◆◆◆◆◆◆◆◆◆◆◆◆◆◆◆◆◆◆◆◆◆◆◆◆◆◆◆◆◆

Imagine yourself in the 1500s

Your task 🖉 ✂️

Choose your favourite picture of the 1500s.

You have been taken back in time. You are standing inside this picture in the 1500s.

1. Draw a **small** picture of yourself standing in your casual weekend clothes.
   Cut the picture out and stick it on to a corner of the picture.
2. Describe what you can see.

Around me I can see _____

_____

_____

3. How do you feel? (Choose some of these words to explain how you feel:
   frightened; amused; excited; bewildered.)

Finding myself in the picture about _____ *I feel*

_____

_____

_____

4. What problems do you face?
   (Think about the strange clothes you are wearing, the different coins in your
   pocket, your watch, walkman and other modern items!)

If I found myself back in the sixteenth century, the people all around me would

_____

_____

3

You will need
- pen or pencil
- scissors
- glue

There are four pages to this task

◆━◆━◆━◆━◆━◆━◆━◆━◆━◆━◆━◆━◆━◆━◆━◆━◆━◆━◆━

┌───┐

◆ **HISTORY DICTIONARY**

The important words   **My explanation of them**

gentlemen   _____

gentlewomen   _____

citizens   _____

yeomen   _____

labourers   _____

                             _____

└───┘

What sorts of people lived in the 1500s?

One person who lived in England during the 1500s said, 'We in England divide our people into four groups: **gentlemen**, **citizens**, **yeomen** and **labourers**.' This person would not have mentioned women in his list because in those days women were not really considered as important!

Gentlemen

Some gentlemen were very rich. They were dukes and earls. They helped the king run the country. Other gentlemen were not quite as rich. They owned large houses and had servants. They had big farms with farmers working for them. They made sure that everyone obeyed the laws of the land.

Their wives were called **gentlewomen**. They ran the household, hired servants and entertained guests.

Citizens

The **citizens** were rich people who lived in towns. Some were merchants who bought and sold cloth and wool. Others were expert craftsmen who worked with gold and silver. They lived in large town houses and had servants. Citizens' wives did not 'go out to work', but ran the household. They would hire all the servants, buy all the food and drink, and organise the family's finances.

Yeomen

The **yeomen** were farmers. They owned or rented land from the gentlemen. They had quite a good life. Their wives helped them on the farm by looking after the vegetable gardens, chickens and goats. They were responsible for the cows and dairy produce. They also kept the household in order, just as the gentry wives did. They sometimes had servants too.

Labourers

Labourers were people who had no land. If they lived in the country they would probably work on farms. If they lived in towns they might be shopkeepers or shoemakers or bricklayers. Their wives and children had to 'muck in' and do just as many of the dirty jobs as the labourers themselves.

3 👉

Your task ✂️ 📄

There are pictures below of the men and women who made up these four groups. There are also pictures of their homes. Unfortunately Ernest Muddle has muddled them all together.

1. Cut out each picture.
2. Match the husbands and wives.
3. Match each couple to a home.
4. Glue them in the right boxes on page 3.

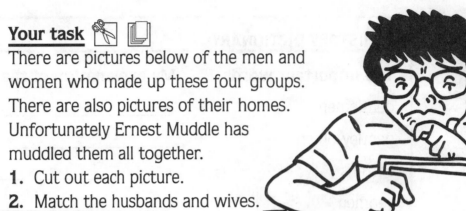

✂️

THE MAKING OF THE UK SUPPORT MATERIALS

3

	The men	Their wives	Their homes
gentleman			
citizen			
yeoman			
labourer			

3

◆-◆

Women in the 1500s

Your task

1. What clues helped you to find the gentlewoman's husband?

_____

_____

_____

2. How was the gentlewoman different from the labourer's wife?

_____

_____

_____

3. How can you tell that yeomen's wives had to work quite hard?

_____

_____

_____

4. How can you tell that gentlemen's wives hardly had to work at all?

_____

_____

_____

4

You will need
- pen or pencil

♦ HISTORY DICTIONARY

The important words	My explanation of them
vagrant	_____
workhouse	_____
the deserving poor	_____
rogue	_____
	_____

Were the poor really poor?

In the sixteenth and seventeenth centuries, the country was full of very poor people. The poorest people had no homes or jobs. They wandered around the country begging. They were known as **vagrants**.

A poor man in torn and tattered clothes, begging outside his house

Other poor people did have homes and jobs. They normally worked on farms or, in the later part of the period, in towns. Their wages were so bad, however, that sometimes they couldn't feed their families. If the crops failed, poor people might starve to death.

The deserving poor

The government decided that there were different types of poor people. Some were truly poor. Perhaps they had lost their jobs? Perhaps they were children whose parents had died? Perhaps they had been injured in the wars? Perhaps they had a dreadful disease? These poor people were the '**deserving poor**'. The government gave them a licence to beg for money. The government and towns also set up **workhouses** and hospitals to help them. The government made people pay taxes to help the deserving poor.

Beggars were given licences, badges and special beggars' bags

Rogues

The government said that some people were just lazy and did not want to work. They said that others had made themselves poor on purpose. They were **rogues**. They did not deserve to be helped. So, if people were caught begging who didn't need to, they were punished.

Beggars being whipped and then hanged

Some of the punishments were very cruel. The beggars could be whipped or put in the stocks. They could have holes drilled through their ears. Some of them had the letter V for vagrant burned on their backs. Some of them were even hanged.

4 ☞

Your task

Use the information on pages 1 and 2 to answer the following questions. Write your answers in the spaces provided.

1. What happened to poor people when the crops failed?

When the crops failed _____

_____

2. List three ways that the government and towns used to try and help the deserving poor.

The government and towns helped the deserving poor by _____

and _____ and _____ .

3. Find four punishments that rogues were given.

Rogues were _____

_____

_____

_____

 Are there very poor people nowadays? If so, how do the government and towns deal with this problem?

4

☞

Your task

1. These pictures show six beggars. Match each written description on the next page with one of the pictures here.

2. In the space underneath each picture, write what that person did to try to get money or food.

A Clapper Dudgeon

_____

_____

_____

The Upright Man

_____

_____

_____

The Doxy

_____

_____

_____

The Counterfeit Crank

_____

_____

_____

Bawdy Baskets

_____

_____

_____

The Abraham Man

_____

_____

_____

THE MAKING OF THE UK SUPPORT MATERIALS

A This beggar walks with a sheet around him. He doesn't wear anything else. He shouts and stares with a wild look and **pretends to be mad**, so that people will give him money.

B This man is the king of vagrants. He doesn't beg but he **demands that people give him money**. He also helps himself to other vagrants' possessions and even to their women.

C This beggar **pretends to be lame**. He has crutches. Sometimes he also sucks soap so that he foams at the mouth. People think he is very ill, so they give him money.

D This man **makes sores on his body** on purpose so people will feel sorry for him and give him money. He puts a salty cloth on his skin. Then he pulls the cloth off. This leaves the skin red raw.

E This woman carries a basket on her arm. There are laces, pins and silk in it. She **steals cloth and sells it** for beef, bacon or cheese.

F This woman carries a backpack full of stolen goods. She **steals chickens** by feeding them with bread tied to a rope. There is a needle on the end of the rope. The chickens choke and she drags them under her cloak.

Do you think that all these people were rogues, who were only pretending to be poor and helpless, or do you think they really were poor and helpless?

4

Here are four sources which describe poor people.

Your task
1. Read each source.
2. Decide whether it is describing the deserving poor or a rogue.
3. Cross out the wrong description.
4. Underline the words or phrases in the source which gave you proof.

SOURCE 1 From a census taken in 1570

Anne Buckle, 46 years old. Widow. Two children, one 9 years old, the other 5 years old. They work lace. Have always lived here. Very poor.

Ann Buckle was

deserving poor / a rogue

SOURCE 2 From Cornwall court records, 1741

Thomas Davy, a vagrant, is a rogue. He is sent to prison to serve with hard labour for three months and also on Saturday next he is to be stripped naked from his middle upwards and be publicly whipped till his body be bloody.

Thomas Davy was

deserving poor / a rogue

SOURCE 3 From a census in 1571

John Burr, 54 years old. Glazier. Very sick and cannot work. Alice his wife that spins. Seven children, the eldest twenty years of age, the youngest two years. They can spin wool. Have always lived here. Very poor.

John Burr was

deserving poor / a rogue

SOURCE 4 From Surrey court records, 1667

Robert Wheeler's house has just blown down. The parish may build a cottage on the wasteland for Wheeler. This cottage will be used for the poor of the parish.

Robert Wheeler was

deserving poor / a rogue

5

You will need
• pen or pencil

Why were people poor?

cause

consequence

Your task A

1. Read these sentences carefully and look at the picture.
2. Now fill in the history dictionary box.

A **cause** is a reason why something happens. For example, too much sunbathing causes people to get sunburnt.
A **consequence** is a result of something that happens. So the consequence of too much sunbathing is that people get sunburnt.

Your task B

In this task you are going to look at reasons why people were poor in the 1500s. You are also going to see how good you are at linking causes and consequences.

1. Get into small groups. Your teacher will give you a set of cards which explain why people were poor. Each card is either a cause or a consequence.
2. Sort your cards into two piles. One should be a set of causes, the other a set of consequences.
3. Match each cause to the right consequence.
4. Discuss with your group what **you** think are the most important causes and consequences of poverty.
5. Place these at the top of the table.
6. Now place the other causes and consequences in order so that the least important ones are at the bottom of the table.

Now...

Look at the way that other groups have sorted their cards. Did they come to the same conclusions as your group, or were their ideas different?

Ask the other groups **why** they put their cards into the order they did.

◆◆◆◆◆◆◆◆◆◆◆◆◆◆◆◆◆◆◆◆◆

Your task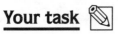
Complete this essay.

Why were people poor?

In my opinion, the most important reason why people were so poor in the sixteenth century was

_____

_____

This was an important reason because

_____

_____

Another reason why people were so poor was

_____

_____

This was also very important because

_____

_____

There were several other reasons why people were so poor, such as

_____

_____

Probably the least important reason why people were poor was

_____

_____

It must have been very _____ being a poor person in those days.

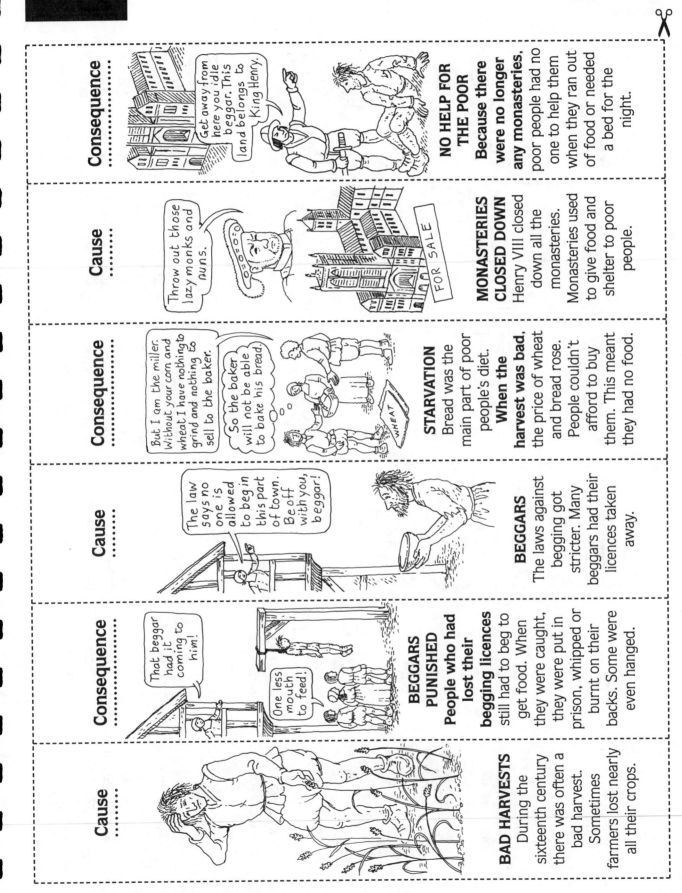

Consequence

Get out of here before I set about whipping your wife and baby as well.

HOMELESSNESS
When poor people **couldn't afford to pay their rent,** the landlord threw them out of their cottages. This meant they were homeless.

Cause

This house you live in costs my master Lord Walton a lot of money. From next month he is raising the rent.

But we can't to pay any more.

RISING RENTS
9 out of 10 people were peasants who had very little money. They lived in tiny cottages which they rented. The rents kept increasing until poor people couldn't afford to pay.

Consequence

I'm sorry. I need this cottage for my new shepherd.

PEASANTS LOSE EVERYTHING!
Fewer men were needed to tend sheep than to grow crops. Many people lost their jobs and also their cottages on the farmers' land.

Consequence

4 bushels of wheat for 200 people = starvation. How are we going to manage?

NOT ENOUGH FOOD
Because there were **so many more people,** there was not enough food for everyone to eat. This meant that the poorest people starved.

Cause

Sheep farming is where the money is. I only need one shepherd instead of five farm labourers.

MORE SHEEP FARMING
Farmers could earn more money breeding sheep to make woollen cloth than growing crops like wheat. Many became 'pastoral' farmers rather than 'arable' farmers.

Cause

When great grandma was alive there were only 20 people in this village. Now there are 200!

RISING POPULATION
During the sixteenth century, the population of England rose quickly. There were hundreds of thousands more people who needed houses, jobs and food.

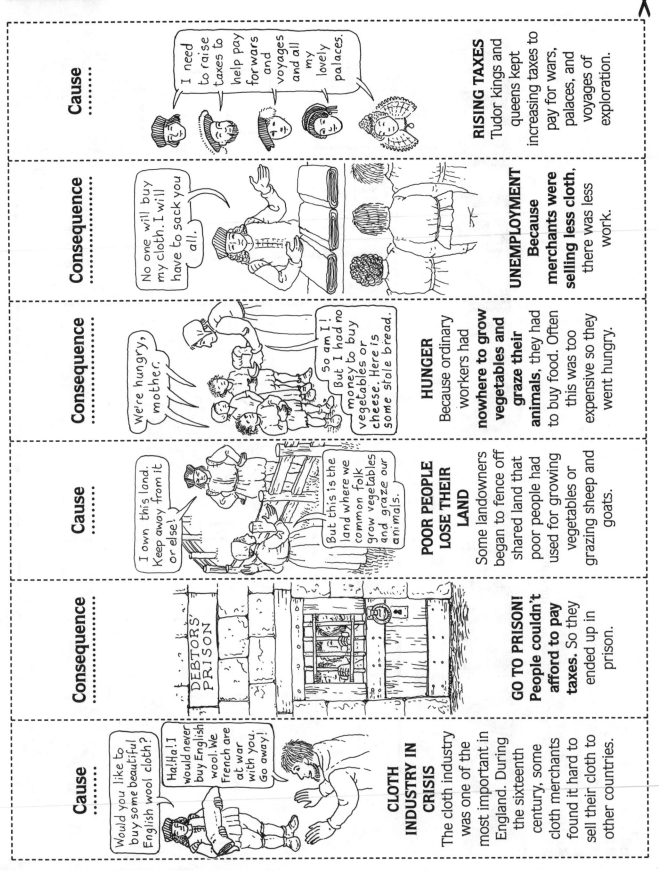

You will need

- 2, 3 or 4
  players
- a dice
- some counters
- a set of
  Poverty
  Pursuits
  question cards

POVERTY PURSUITS

How to play

■ Throw a six to start.
■ Each player throws the dice in turn.
■ If you land on a ? another player selects one of the question cards and reads out the question.
■ If you get the answer right, take another turn.
■ If you get the answer wrong, miss a turn.
■ The first person to reach the finish wins the game.

Copy these on to coloured card.

Question
What was the main part of a poor person's diet?
Answer
Bread

Question
What happened to people when they couldn't afford to pay their rent?
Answer
The landlord threw them out of their cottages.

Question
Who did the government describe as rogues?
Answer
People who they said had made themselves poor on purpose and did not want to work.

Question
Describe at least one thing that happened when beggars were caught begging without a licence.
Answer
■ They were put in prison; or
■ They were whipped; or
■ They were burnt on their back; or
■ They were hanged.

Question
Who were the deserving poor?
Answer
People who were poor through no fault of their own – because they had lost their jobs, for example.

Question
What was a beggar's licence?
Answer
A piece of paper given to some poor people giving them permission to beg.

Question
Give one reason why the Tudor kings and queens kept raising taxes.
Answer
■ To pay for wars; or
■ To pay for voyages of exploration; or
■ To pay for palaces.

Question
When did the price of wheat and bread rise?
Answer
When the harvest failed.

Question
How many English people were peasants?
Answer
9 out of 10.

Copy these on to coloured card.

Question
How did monks and nuns try to help the poor?
Answer
By giving them food and a place to stay.

Question
Growing crops is called 'arable' farming. What is sheep farming called?
Answer
Pastoral farming.

Question
What did some landlords do to the common land?
Answer
They put fences round it.

Question
Did the population of England rise or fall during the sixteenth century?
Answer
The population rose.

Question
Why did some English cloth workers lose their jobs?
Answer
Because some countries stopped buying English cloth.

Question
What did the letter V stand for when it was burned on someone's back?
Answer
V for vagrant.

Question
Who closed down the monasteries?
Answer
Henry VIII.

Question
Does sheep farming employ more or fewer workers than arable farming?
Answer
Fewer.

Question
Give one reason why a poor family might have no flour to bake bread.
Answer
■ A bad harvest; or
■ Shared land fenced off by a landowner; or
■ They had no money to buy food.

There are two pages to this task

7

You will need
- pen or pencil
- paper

Finding out about private lives

Long ago historians were mostly interested in kings and queens, wars and disasters. Hardly anyone wrote about the lives of ordinary men, women and children.

Your task

1. Discuss this question in a small group.

Why do you think historians from long ago did not write about the private lives of ordinary men, women and children?

2. Write down your answers in the space below.
3. Share your answers with the rest of the class.

Reasons why historians did not write about the private lives of ordinary men, women and children

_____

_____

_____

_____

_____

Nowadays things are different. Some historians are interested in ordinary people and their daily lives. However, they have a problem. If they had wanted to study kings and queens there would be a lot of evidence available. If they want to study ordinary people and their private lives, there is not much evidence.

Your task

1. Make a list on a separate sheet of paper of all the ways in which you the historian could find out about the life of a rich and famous king such as Henry VIII. You could start like this:

Ways in which we could find out about King Henry VIII
Go to an art gallery and study his portrait.

2. Imagine you are historians in the year AD 2095 (about 100 years' time). You want to find out what teenagers were like in the 1990s. You will want to know about what teenagers ate, what they wore, what life was like at school and what they did in their spare time.
Make a list of sources of evidence you would look for. You could start like this:

Evidence which will help a historian to find out about a typical teenager from the 1990s

What they ate	What they wore	What life was like at school	What they did in their spare time
			A list of the Top 20 from a 1990s pop magazine.

Why are these two lists so different?
Would any of the sources of evidence be the same?

8

Getting married

One modern historian has spent many years trying to find out about the lives of ordinary people from long ago. His name is Lawrence Stone. He is very interested in the reasons why people got married. He claims that in 1500 parents usually chose who their children got married to. He says that by 1750 people were choosing their own husbands or wives. He claims that his evidence shows just how much people's view of marriage had changed in 250 years.

You are going to use some evidence to see if you agree with Lawrence Stone. Had things changed?

Your task

Examine the timeline on the next page. It has the names of different people who got married between 1450 and 1750. The written sources on the timeline tell you that some of these people chose to get married and some of them were forced to get married.

1. Read each source carefully.
2. Decide whether this person chose who to marry for themselves or whether their parents chose for them. Write YES or NO in the space provided.
3. In the final column, write what evidence there is in the source to support your view.
4. Does the evidence from this timeline and these sources prove that Lawrence Stone was right or wrong? Explain your answer carefully.

◆◆

Date	Name of person	Source	Did they choose for themselves? Yes or No	Evidence in the source to support your conclusion
1450	Elizabeth Paston	[When Elizabeth had refused to marry the man her parents had chosen] She has since Easter been beaten once or twice in the week, and had her head broken in two or three places. Letter from Elizabeth's mother	NO	Elizabeth's mum hit her because she didn't want to get married. This means she was probably forced to get married.
1599	Margerie Shaftoe	I give my daughter Margerie in marriage to Edward son of Reynold Shaftoe. Will of William Shaftoe		
1681	Mary Josselin	My daughter Mary rejected Mr Rhea [as a husband]. He seemed not loving to her. I was sad but did not want to make both their lives miserable. Diary of Ralph Josselin		
1719	The Duke of Richmond's son	The marriage of the Duke's son was made to pay off money the Duke had lost through gambling. The son was sent home from school and the girl from the nursery. They were immediately man and wife A biography of the Duke of Richmond		

8

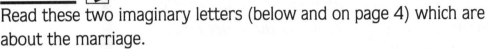

Arranged marriages

There is a lot of evidence that rich families often arranged the marriages of their children. Sometimes one family agreed to marry into another family to help pay off debts. The Duke of Richmond decided to 'marry his son off' because he lost all his money playing cards!

Your task

Read these two imaginary letters (below and on page 4) which are about the marriage.

February 14th 1719

To my dearest wife,

You will be pleased to know that the small matter of my debt to Lord Pembroke has been settled. We have agreed that there should be a marriage between the two families. He has a daughter aged nine. I forget what she is called. I told him that we have three sons. We agreed that, because my gambling debt was less than £500, it would be all right for us to offer our middle son Tom in marriage. We will save our eldest son for a more important marriage.

Will you arrange matters with the minister from the church?

I hope all is well with you. I have business affairs in London, so will be away for another three months.

Your loving husband

Henry.

To my dearest son,

As you know, your father loves you dearly. He has arranged for you to marry the daughter of Lord Pembroke. Even at nine years old, she is more beautiful than her sisters. Her father is very rich. This marriage will make you very rich too. You are lucky to have a father who works so hard to look after the family.

I know you will learn to love her, just as I grew to love your father.

The wedding is arranged for Monday week. The masters at school will arrange for you to come home. I have hired a tutor so you can continue your lessons whilst you are here.

Your loving mother

Beatrice.

Your task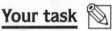

Imagine you are either Tom, or the nine-year-old girl. It is the day after the wedding. You only saw each other for a few minutes whilst the ceremony took place. Then you were both taken back home again. On the next page write a letter to your best friend telling them your true feelings about the wedding.

■ You could begin by explaining what has happened.
■ You could describe how you felt when you saw the other person.
■ You could tell them what the minister said.
■ You could say how you feel about your parents.

To my dearest friend,

_____

_____

_____

_____

_____

_____

_____

_____

_____

_____

_____

_____

I hope all is well with you

Yours ever,

Thynke on mee.

9

You will need

- pen or pencil
- coloured pencils

Being married

Being married has never been easy. In the sixteenth and seventeenth centuries there were some happy marriages and some unhappy marriages, just like today.

One thing that was different in the sixteenth and seventeenth centuries was that husbands had much more power over their wives than they have today. When a woman got married, everything she owned became her husband's. Men were even allowed to hit their wives as long as the stick was no thicker than a man's thumb.

Some men said very unkind things about women. Women were not allowed to answer back.

Your task

1. Read this written source about women.
2. There are three words which mean 'gossip' or 'talking too much'. Can you find them?

> **SOURCE 1** From a sermon given by Bishop Aylmer in the sixteenth century
>
> *Women are of two sorts. Some of them are wiser and better than men, but some are foolish flibbergibs, tattlers, witless, feeble, proud dainty tale bearers, rumour raisers and in every way doltified with the dregs of the devil's dunghill.*

Men often criticised their wives for gossiping. If a man thought his wife was talking too much, he could make her wear a scold's bridle. This was a metal cage which was put over the woman's head. A long spike stuck into her mouth. This stopped her from talking. It also made her feel as though she was choking to death. It must have been a horrible punishment.

S in C pp. 18–19   *THE MAKING OF THE UK SUPPORT MATERIALS*

9

☞

page 2

◆━◆━◆━◆━◆━◆━◆━◉━◆━◆━◆━◆━◆━◆━◆

'Wife sales' were common among ordinary people. These were a kind of divorce. Both the husband and wife would agree to it and the wife would accept a new husband.

Your task 📋 ✏️

1. Read this description of a wife sale.

> **SOURCE 2** Written in the 1740s
>
> *The husband puts a halter (rope) about her neck and leads her up to the next market place. He puts her up to be sold to the best bidder, as if she were a horse. A buyer is usually arranged beforehand.*

2. Design a poster advertising your wife for sale.
Use the outline on the next page to help you.
Your poster could include
■ a description of your wife and what she looks like
■ an explanation of why you want to sell her
■ a list of her good points
■ a list of her bad points
■ how much you want to sell her for.

Here are some words and phrases you might like to use.

My wife	is foolish	is a flibbergib	has a devilish manner
scratches and bites	is feeble	is a rumour raiser	
is doltified with the dregs of the devil's dunghill		is stubborn	is proud
My wife is	constant	wise	dainty	generous	obedient
a home lover	loving	good-humoured	

💬 **Why would the husband have to write good things about his wife as well as bad things?**
How do you think women reacted when their husbands acted like this?

◆◆◆

10

Being married – a woman's viewpoint

You will need
- pen or pencil
- picture sources

We can find out quite a lot about people's marriages from diaries and letters. But often they only give us one side of the story – usually the man's. We have to use our imagination to think about what the woman's point of view might have been.

Your task A

1. Read the source on the next page. It was written by a man called Samuel Pepys. He wrote a private diary. He wrote about how he felt.
2. When you have read it, underline all the words and phrases which describe Samuel fighting with his wife.
3. Imagine you are Pepys' wife Elizabeth. What would **she** have written in **her** diary for each of these days? Use the lines next to Samuel's diary to write her version.

Your task B

1. Look through the picture sources in the Picture Pack for examples of married women.
2. Choose one woman and describe her. Is she at home? Is she working?

_____

_____

3. Use the evidence in the picture source to imagine what kind of life and marriage she might have had.

I think this woman had a _____ marriage. The reason I think this is

_____

◆▬◆▬◆▬◆▬◆▬◆▬◆▬◆▬◆▬◆▬◆▬◆▬◆▬◆

Samuel Pepys' Diary	Elizabeth Pepys' Diary
2 May 1663 I slept till almost 7 o'clock. So up and to my office (having had some angry words with my wife about her neglecting to keep the house clean, I calling her a 'beggar' and she calling me a 'prick louse'). Returned home to dinner. Very merry and well pleased with my wife.	
19 December 1664 I was very angry and began to find fault with my wife for not commanding the servants as she ought. She gave me an angry answer. I did strike her over her left eye such a blow as the poor wretch did cry out. But her spirit was such that she scratched and bit me.	
12 July 1667 …And so home and there finding my wife in a bad mood for my not dining at home, I did give her a pull by the nose. I decided to go back to the office to avoid further anger.	

11

You will need

- pen or pencil
- Happy Family cards

◆ HISTORY DICTIONARY

The important words	My explanation of them
wet nurse	_____
	_____
	_____

Having children

In the sixteenth and seventeenth centuries, people did not know about germs. They did not understand that germs caused illness, so they drank dirty water. They did not wash as often as we do and they sometimes dressed in dirty clothes. There was no electricity, no central heating and no disinfectant. There were no drugs or painkillers and no antibiotics.

Not surprisingly, people caught many dreadful diseases. Babies and children were particularly at risk. Often, babies died almost as soon as they were born. Children became sick and, because there were no antibiotics to give them, they died too. There were no vaccinations, so when there were measles or mumps epidemics, thousands of children died.

Your task

In groups of three or four, you are going to play the 'Happy Families' game. Each of you is either the mother or father of a family. You have had ten children. In this game you will find out how many of your children survived and how many died.

1. Take the set of Happy Family cards and place them face down on the desk.
2. Each person picks one card in turn. Read it out to the rest of your group. It will tell you about one of your children. Did they live or did they die?
3. Write the name of the child and whether they died or survived on your 'Happy Family' score sheet on the next page.

When the game is over, find out which of you had the most survivors. Did any of you find that nearly all your children died? This sometimes happened. For example, Catherine of Aragon, who was Henry VIII's first wife, had eight children. Only one of them, Mary, survived.

☞

Happy Families score card (How will your family get on in the game of survival?)

Family name _____

(Choose a name you could use – your own or invent one)

Child's name	Child's name	Child's name	Child's name	Child's name
Died or survived? ____	Died or survived? ____	Died or survived? ____	Died or survived? ____	Died or survived? ____

Child's name	Child's name	Child's name	Child's name	Child's name
Died or survived? ____	Died or survived? ____	Died or survived? ____	Died or survived? ____	Died or survived? ____

Ten children were born in our family. _____ children died, and _____ children survived.

◆◆◆◆◆◆◆◆◆◆◆◆◆◆◆◆◆◆◆◆◆◆◆◆◆◆◆◆◆◆◆◆◆◆◆◆

You are now going to describe what happened to you in the game.

Your task

Either:

a) Write a letter to your long-lost cousin. Describe what has happened to you in your life. You could tell him or her:

■ how many children you had

■ what happened to them all

■ which of the children who died was your favourite and how you felt when they died.

Or:

b) Complete the outline of the family portrait below. In the original picture the father is looking at skulls which show how many of his children died. Put the correct number of skulls at the back to show how many of your children died. Put the correct number of children at the front to show the children who survived.

Add labels to your picture to explain who the children are and what happened to them.

👉

Your task 📓 ✏️

1. Look through all the Happy Family cards which tell you about children who died. There are 24 of them. Pick out the cards with these names: Amy; Margaret; Mark; Ann.

2. Find four sources or pieces of information on pages 20 and 21 of *Societies in Change* that are similar to these cards. If you do not have that book, your teacher will give you a sheet of sources.

3. Complete this chart:

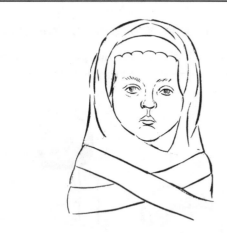

Amy's story was similar to

_____

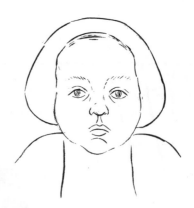

Margaret's story was similar to

_____

Ann's story was similar to

_____

Mark's story was similar to

_____

Copy these on to coloured card.

✂

The midwife used forceps at your son Mark's birth. His right eye was damaged. He was so ugly that you sent him to live with his grandparents who neglected him and he died.

Your three-year-old son James was playing in the kitchens. He ate some rat poison and died.

Your four-year-old son Paul was beaten so hard by his father that he fell down the stairs and died.

There was an outbreak of measles in the servants' quarters. Your daughter Beth was infected and died.

Your daughter Margaret had to wear an iron corset, even though she was only three years old. One day she fell over. The corset was so tight that she couldn't catch her breath. She died.

The wet nurse drank too much. One day, as she was feeding your son Simon, she was so drunk that she rolled on top of him. He was squashed to death.

When your baby Amy was three months old, the wet nurse left her hanging on a rusty nail. Amy scraped her head on the nail and caught an infection. She died a week later.

Your two-year-old son Ben choked to death on a chicken bone.

Your baby boy was born two months early and died within a few hours.

You had a baby daughter who was sickly. Her name was Ann but nobody really wanted her. You had hoped for a boy. She died of neglect.

Copy these on to coloured card.

There was a fire in the nearby barn. Your son Joseph, who was only two, wandered down there and was choked to death by the smoke.

Your five-year-old daughter Emma wandered into the kitchen. She tripped over the firewood basket and fell against the bread oven. Her burns were so bad that she died.

You were angry that your newborn baby was a girl, so you smothered (killed) her with a pillow when nobody was looking.

The family decided to move house. As the servants were lifting your newborn son Henry's cradle, they didn't realise he was still inside. He fell out and landed on his head. He died instantly.

Your one-year-old son Matthew drowned in the village duckpond.

Your three-year-old son Tim was mauled by a mongrel dog. He died of his wounds.

Your four-year-old daughter Alice fell into the stream at the end of the garden. She caught pneumonia and died.

An outbreak of plague killed your five-year-old daughter Joanna.

You took your newborn baby Lucy to visit her grandparents. Unfortunately you were caught in a freak thunderstorm. She caught a chill and died.

Your baby boy was stillborn (born dead).

THE MAKING OF THE UK SUPPORT MATERIALS

Copy these on to coloured card.

Your seven-year-old son Christopher is about to start school. He is a fine, healthy specimen who has never had a day's illness.

Your sixteen-year-old daughter Mary is always complaining that she is bored. You hope that she will soon realise that her place is at home with her mother. She should stop complaining.

Your two-year-old daughter Kathryn wandered away from the house. She was found three weeks later at the bottom of an old well.

Your eldest son Charles is now twenty-five. He is getting married next week to your best friend's daughter.

Your sister's family was so jealous of the arrival of your new baby son Jacob, that they arranged for one of the servants to creep into his bedroom and strangle him.

Your ten-year-old daughter Hannah is a real treasure. She is slightly deaf after an attack of German measles, but no one really notices and she can lip read very well.

Your baby daughter Jane caught smallpox and died.

Your newborn baby Francis weighs a healthy eight pounds. He eats and sleeps so much that you know he is strong and fit.

Your baby son William was born with only one ear. The midwife said he was the devil's son. You could not find a wet nurse to feed him so he died of neglect.

Your daughter Helen is twenty now. Although she had mumps as a child, she survived. You hope she will make a good marriage in a few years' time.

Copy these on to coloured card.

Your daughter Louise is twenty-three years old now. She is thinking of marrying the local physician. He is a good man, so you are very happy for her.

Your daughter Rachel is a wonderful housewife. Anyone who has aches and pains goes to her for help. She is still only fourteen but seems to know such a lot about herbal cures.

You are thanking God for the safe delivery from plague of your six-month-old daughter Rose.

Your son Roger is the image of his father, even though he is still only eight years old. He says he wants to be a wool merchant too, just like his father and elder brother.

Although your son Daniel had three fingers of his left hand bitten off by a dog when he was six, it hasn't stopped him growing into a very handsome teenager.

Your daughter Susannah can sometimes be very noisy, but you are just happy that she is alive. You hate thinking about what happened when she was six, and nearly got eaten by a circus bear...

You are sure that your twelve-year-old daughter Agnes will survive until adulthood. After all, she recovered from a dreadful attack of scarlet fever and pneumonia, thank the Lord.

Your daughter Martha is a credit to the family. Even though she is only nine years old, she can stitch and sew beautifully.

Your seventeen-year-old son Stephen is your pride and joy. He is determined to enter his father's wool merchant's business and make the family fortune.

Your son Samuel is thinking of becoming a vicar. You are sure he will make a fine job of it. However, you have asked him to wait another five years until he is twenty.

Having children – more information

SOURCE 1

Children as young as three or four were dressed as little adults. Daughters in rich families were encased in corsets reinforced with iron. This was intended to make sure they walked gracefully, but their lungs were sometimes damaged.

SOURCE 2 Sir Simonds d'Ewes writing about his childhood

December 1602 – *bungled delivery damaged his right eye at birth – could never use it for reading.*
5 months old – *sent to wet nurse for several months.*
1–8 years old – *sent to grandfather's house. Grandparents not there so brought up by servants – parents only visited him twice.*
8 years old – *sent to boarding school.*

SOURCE 3 William Blundell reports on the birth and death of his sixth daughter in 1653

My wife has much disappointed my hopes by bringing forth a daughter, which, finding itself not so welcome in this world as a son, hath departed.

SOURCE 4 From a book on childcare written by Dr Cadogan in 1748. It includes this criticism of how wet nurses looked after babies

When [the baby] cries, he is hung from a nail like a bundle of old clothes and while the nurse attends to her business the child remains thus crucified. All who have been found in this situation had a purple face because the blood could not circulate. The baby was believed to be content because he did not have the strength to cry out.

12

There are seven pages to this task

You will need

- pen or pencil
- Picture Source 3
- coloured pencils

Could you enjoy yourself in the sixteenth and seventeenth centuries?

Nowadays, nearly everybody takes part in some sort of sport. The PE department at your school probably offers football, netball, rugby, hockey, dance, swimming and gymnastics. Perhaps it offers other things too? Some of the sports which we enjoy nowadays have been around for hundreds of years.

Your task

1. Make a list of all the games and sporting activities you can think of that people like to do nowadays. (You could try to think of a sport for every single letter of the alphabet!)

Sports and activities which are enjoyed nowadays

A ______	N ______
B ______	O ______
C ______	P ______
D ______	Q ______
E ______	R ______
F ______	S ______
G ______	T ______
H ______	U ______
I ______	V ______
J ______	W ______
K ______	X ______
L ______	Y ______
M ______	Z ______

👉

<u>**Your task**</u> 🔍 ✏️

Look at Source 1. It is a picture made in 1636. It shows people enjoying many different games. These people are not all rich gentlemen – some of them are ordinary people. Here is a list of the games we can see in the picture. Put the names of the games in the right boxes. (Some of the really strange words have already been put in for you!)

throwing the bar   throwing the sledgehammer   leaping   shin kicking   sword fighting   cudgels   headstands   picnicking   fox hunting   hare coursing   dancing   fireworks   horse riding

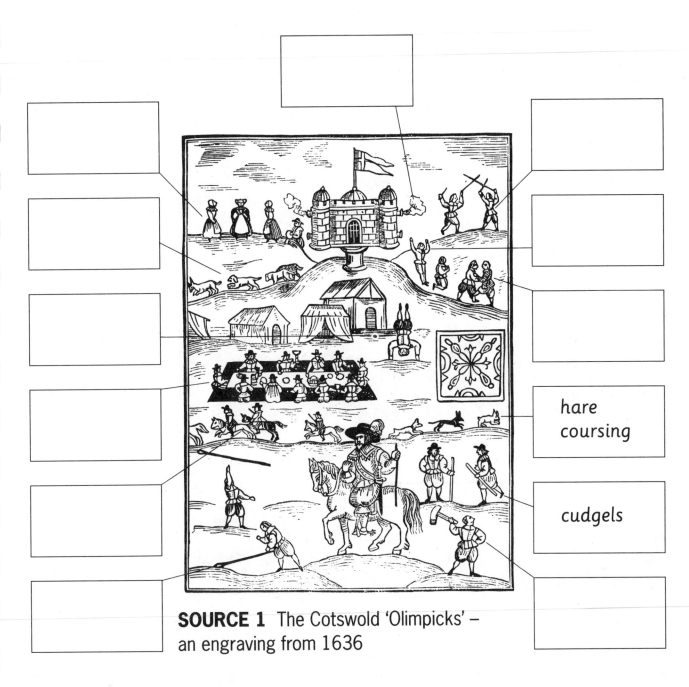

hare coursing

cudgels

SOURCE 1 The Cotswold 'Olimpicks' – an engraving from 1636

12 ☛

Your task

Source 2 below tells you what kinds of sports and pastimes the rich gentlemen from long ago used to enjoy.

1. Read Source 2.
2. The pictures below show some of the activities described in the source. Write the correct activity under each picture. There is an example below.

SOURCE 2 Written by Edwarde Chamberlayne in the seventeenth century

The nobility and gentry have their horse races, hunting, coursing, fishing, hawking, cock fighting, shooting birds, tennis, bowling, billiards, stage plays, dancing and all sorts of musical instruments.

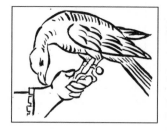   

hawking _____ _____ _____ _____

_____ _____ _____ _____

   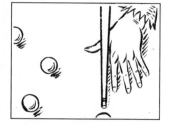

_____ _____ _____ _____

THE MAKING OF THE UK SUPPORT MATERIALS

12

◆◆◆◆◆◆◆◆◆◆◆◆◆◆◆◆◆◆◆◆◆◆◆◆◆◆

☞

Your task

1. Work in small groups. You are going to write a quiz for another group. Look at Picture Source 3 from the Picture Pack and write 10 questions about it. You could ask questions such as 'How many people are doing the conga?' or 'Where is the man doing a headstand?'.
2. Pass your quiz to another group for them to fill in the answers.

Questions   **Answers**

1. _____   _____

   _____   _____

2. _____   _____

   _____   _____

3. _____   _____

   _____   _____

4. _____   _____

   _____   _____

5. _____   _____

   _____   _____

6. _____   _____

   _____   _____

7. _____   _____

   _____   _____

8. _____   _____

9. _____   _____

10. _____   _____

 What kinds of people are shown enjoying themselves in this picture?

12

◆◆◆◆◆◆◆◆◆◆◆◆◆◆◆◆◆◆◆◆◆◆◆◆◆◆◆◆◆◆◆◆◆◆◆◆◆◆

Your task

1. What were the main differences between the sports played by the nobles and the sports played by the ordinary people?

_____

_____

_____

2. Why do you think the nobles played different games from the ordinary people?

_____

_____

_____

_____

3. Look at your list of games we play nowadays. Write down any which the evidence shows people played long ago as well as nowadays.

_____

_____

_____

_____

Do you think that people's ways of enjoying themselves have changed a great deal since the sixteenth and seventeenth centuries?
Do you think that people _did_ enjoy themselves in the sixteenth and seventeenth centuries?

12

page 6

Bull baiting

Your task

1. Read Source 3. It was written in the late seventeenth century.

SOURCE 3 From Misson's *Memoirs and Observations*

They tie a rope to the horns of a bull and fasten the other end to an iron ring fixed to a stake. They let loose one of the dogs. The dog runs round the bull, trying to get beneath his belly.

The bull's chief aim is to slide a horn under the dog's belly and to throw it so high it will break its neck in the fall. This often happens. Sometimes the dog is thrown 30 feet high and this puts him in danger of a damnable squelch when he comes down.

---

2. What would a person from nowadays think of a sport like this?

_____

_____

_____

3. What would a person from the seventeenth century think of a sport like this?

_____

_____

_____

4. Why do you think their views would be so different?

_____

_____

_____

THE MAKING OF THE UK SUPPORT MATERIALS

12

Your task

You are planning the entertainments for your village feast day in the seventeenth century. Choose one of the entertainments you have found out about and make a poster to advertise it. Think about who it would appeal to and why they might like it.

✳✳✳ FEAST DAY ENTERTAINMENT ✳✳✳

13

There are five pages to this task

◆◆◆◆◆◆◆◆◆◆◆◆◆◆◆◆◆◆◆◆◆◆◆◆◆◆◆◆

You will need
- pen or pencil

◆ **HISTORY DICTIONARY**

The important words	My explanation of them
Catholic	_____
mass	_____
tithes	_____
baptism	_____
confirmation	_____
last rites	_____
purgatory	_____

What religion did people follow in 1500?

The mass

In 1500 England was still a **Catholic** country. Everyone went to church on Sunday to attend **mass** and take communion. This meant they ate bread and drank wine. The Catholic religion taught them that this was the body and blood of Jesus. They also gave some of their money to church (a **tithe**). Nearly everyone still believed that if you did not go to mass or did not pay your tithes it was a sin and God would punish you.

The Church also helped you at special times through your life.

Baptism

When you were born your parents had you baptised by the priest. **Baptism** cleaned all your sins away. This meant that everyone started their life completely free from sin!

Confirmation

The Church tried to help you again when you were about twelve years old. This time, the bishop confirmed you. **Confirmation** was very important. It gave you the power to fight the devil and to be good. It also made you a proper member of the Catholic Church.

Marriage

The Church was there again at your wedding. You had to stand in front of a priest and promise to love, honour and obey each other. You had to agree to keep the laws of the Catholic Church too. This was called making your marriage vows.

Last rites

Finally, when you were dying, the priest would visit you and give you the **last rites**. This meant that when you died, you would not go to hell.

Purgatory

When you died, you went to a place called **purgatory**. This was like a waiting room for heaven. If you had only committed a few sins during your life, you only had to stay a short time in purgatory. But if you had committed a lot of sins, you had to spend years and years in purgatory.

The Church taught that if people gave gifts to the Church or to poor people whilst they were alive, this would reduce the time they would spend in purgatory. People could also pay to have extra masses said for them after they died. Of course only the rich could afford to do this.

Your task

Richard Berne was born in London in 1485. He was very wealthy. When he died, his body was buried in a chapel that he had built in St Magnus' Church in London. On page 3 there is an outline of Richard's tomb. In the panels on the side, tell the story of his life in the church. Use words, or draw a picture, to show what happened to Richard Berne at each stage of his life. The information on pages 1 and 2 will help you.

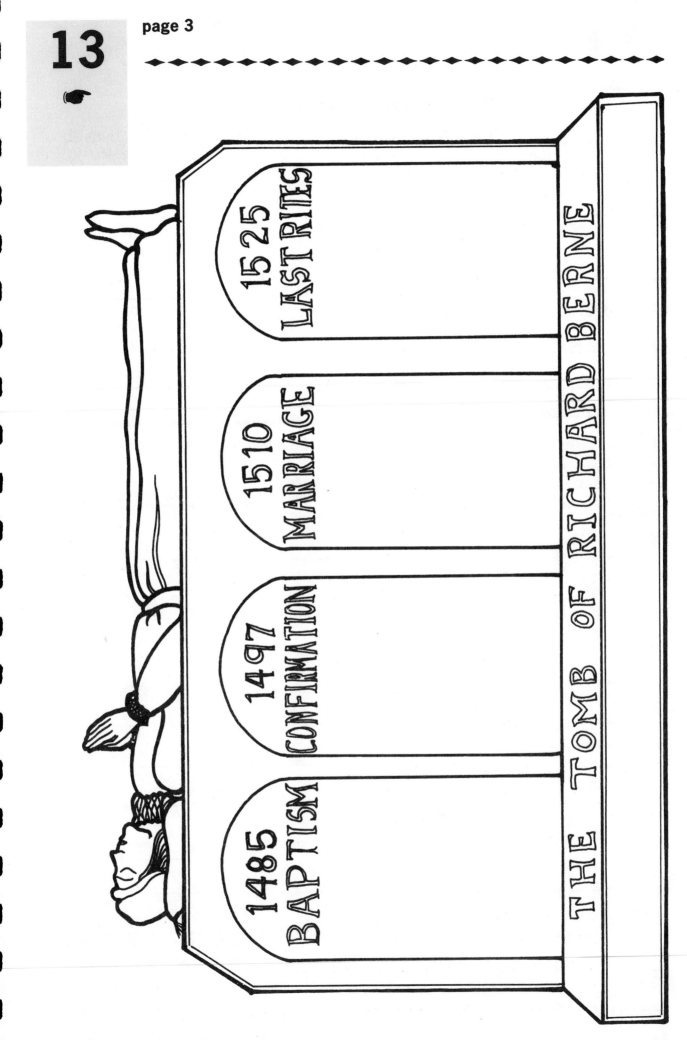

1485 BAPTISM

1497 CONFIRMATION

1510 MARRIAGE

1525 LAST RITES

THE TOMB OF RICHARD BERNE

☞

The will of Richard Berne

Source 1 is part of Richard Berne's will. A will gives instructions about what should happen when someone dies.

Your task 📋 ✏️

1. Read Source 1. Richard Berne did some very kind and good things. Underline them.

SOURCE 1 The will of Richard Berne, London 1525

My body is to be buried in the... chapel that I made in St. Magnus' Church.

For tithes forgotten 3s 4d.

For masses to be said for my soul, my wife's soul and all Christian souls every month for one year after my death: £6.

Every Friday for a year after my death 3s 4d to be given to prisoners in Newgate one Friday, those in Ludgate the next Friday.

The very best canvas for shirts and smocks for the poor people in Bedfordshire.

£100 for the making of an altar table.

---

2. How does Richard's will prove that he believed in the Catholic Church? Explain your answer carefully.

_____

_____

_____

_____

3. How do we know that Richard Berne did **not** want to spend much time in purgatory?

_____

_____

_____

_____

◆━◆━◆━◆━◆━◆━◆━◆━◆━◆━◆━◆━◆━◆━◆━◆━◆

Source 2 is a list of gifts that rich people gave to a church in Suffolk.

SOURCE 2 From a list of church goods in Melford in 1529

A chalice (wine cup for mass), the gift of Mawt Barker, gold 21 ounces.

A piece of the pillar that Christ was tied to, the gift of Sir William Clopton.

A silver pot, the gift of Mother Barrel.

Two silver candlesticks, the gift of old John Smith, 61 ounces.

Total of 80 ornaments, rings and crucifixes.

An altar cloth of silk with blue birds, bordered with blue velvet.

Total of 20 copes and vestments (types of priests' clothing)

A mass book, the gift of John Hill.

Your task

1. Use the evidence in Source 2 to complete this chart.

Church goods   **Given by**

_____

_____

_____

_____

_____

Some unknown people

_____

_____

2. How does Source 2 prove that people still believed in the Catholic Church in 1500?

_____

_____

14

◆ **HISTORY DICTIONARY**

The important words   **My explanation of them**

Protestant

_____

_____

Who were the Protestants?

The evidence suggests that many ordinary people in England were quite happy with the Catholic Church in 1500.

However, there were others who were not happy with the Catholic Church. They protested against it. Because of their protests, they became known as **Protestants**.

Your task

Draw a line to connect each protest about the Catholic Church with a cartoon showing that protest.

Protest 1

They said that the Catholic Church was too rich. People gave lots of money to it but the Church kept the money instead of using it to help the poor. They said priests and monks lived in luxury.

Protest 2

They said that Catholic priests were lazy and did not do their job properly. They said that some priests never even visited their parishes, leaving someone else to take the services.

Protest 3

They said it was wrong that Catholic services and the Bible were still in Latin. Protestants said it was difficult to feel close to God if you couldn't understand or read the Bible yourself.

Protest 4

Protestants were particularly angry that the Catholic Church allowed rich people to pay a bishop or the Pope to have their sins forgiven. They said that only God could forgive sins.

15

You will need
- pen or pencil

What is King Henry VIII famous for?

King Henry VIII was King of England from 1509 to 1547. He is usually remembered for two things:

1. He was the king who had six wives.

2. He was the king who began the changes which turned England into a Protestant country.

Why did he need six wives?

King Henry kept changing his wives for one reason only. He wanted a son who could become king after he died. Look at the pictures below to see what happened.

King Henry VIII

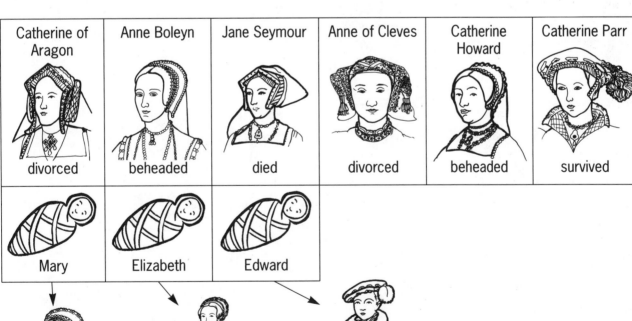
My first wife Catherine had eight children. But they all died except one daughter, Mary. So I divorced her. My second wife, Anne, had another girl – Elizabeth – so I executed her. My third wife Jane had a boy – Edward. But then she died. The other three wives were completely useless! They didn't give me any children at all.

Catherine of Aragon	Anne Boleyn	Jane Seymour	Anne of Cleves	Catherine Howard	Catherine Parr
divorced	beheaded	died	divorced	beheaded	survived
Mary	Elizabeth	Edward			

Princess Mary, Henry's first child

Princess Elizabeth, Henry's second child

Prince Edward, Henry's third child

Why did King Henry quarrel with the Pope?

As you have already found out, King Henry wanted a son so much that he decided to divorce his first wife Catherine of Aragon. He had to ask the Pope for permission because the Pope was the leader of the Catholic Church. The Pope said no.

So King Henry decided to ignore the Pope and make himself head of the Church of England. Then he gave himself a divorce!

Henry hired Protestant teachers for his son Edward. They taught Edward that the Pope was evil and wicked. They gave him Protestant books which said that the Catholic Church was the Church of the devil, not of Christ.

When King Henry died in 1547, his son Edward became King of England and head of the Church of England. He was only nine years old, but he announced that England was now a Protestant country. He said that everyone had to go to Protestant churches. He made sure that all his advisers were Protestant.

15

☞

Your task 📖 ✏️

Use the information on the previous two pages to make a quiz for your friends. Think of three **easy** questions about King Henry and three **hard** questions.

Write the questions here.

QUESTIONS

_____

_____

_____

_____

_____

_____

Leave a space for the answers.

ANSWERS

_____

_____

_____

_____

_____

_____

Put the real answers upside down here.

_____ 6.

_____ 5.

_____ 4.

_____ 3.

_____ 2.

_____ 1.

Now test your friends or your teacher!

There are four pages to this task

16

You will need

- pen or pencil
- coloured pencils

What is Queen Mary famous for?

When King Edward died in 1553, his eldest sister Mary became Queen of England. First of all Mary married Philip, the Catholic King of Spain. Then she announced that England was now a Catholic country again. Next she said that everyone had to go to Catholic churches again. Finally Mary made sure that all her advisers were Catholics.

Queen Mary is usually remembered for two things:

1. She had 284 Protestants burnt to death. This earned her the nickname of 'Bloody Queen Mary'.

2. She was desperate to have children but kept having miscarriages.

Bloody Queen Mary

Source 1 is a picture of two Protestant bishops, Latimer and Ridley, being burned to death. Source 2 (on the next page) is a description of what happened to them.

SOURCE 1 An engraving showing the execution of Latimer and Ridley

S in C pp. 32–33   *THE MAKING OF THE UK SUPPORT MATERIALS*

☞

Your task 📑 ✏️

1. Read Source 2. It was written by a man called John Foxe. He was a Protestant.
2. Underline all the words and phrases in Source 2 which make you think John Foxe was on the same side as the men who were being burned.

SOURCE 2 From John Foxe's *Book of Martyrs*

So they came to the stake... Dr Ridley, seeing Mr Latimer, said, 'Be of good heart brother, for God will either ease the fury of the flames or else strengthen us to endure it.
(Don't worry, everything will be all right, God will help us!)

Dr Ridley gave presents of small things to men standing near, many of whom were weeping strongly.

They brought a lighted faggot (stick) and laid it at Dr Ridley's feet. Then Mr Latimer said 'Do not worry, Mr Ridley. Today, by God's grace, we shall light such a candle in England that it will never go out.

When Ridley saw the fire flame up, he leaned himself to that side. As soon as the fire touched the gunpowder he was seen to stir no more.

---

3. How do you think Queen Mary would have described the scene? Write her description here, using the picture (Source 1) to help you.

_____

_____

_____

_____

_____

_____

_____

_____

☞

Mary, Mary quite contrary

People made up a cruel rhyme about Mary. It went:

Mary, Mary quite contrary	1
How does your garden grow?	2
With silver bells	3
And cockle shells	4
And pretty maids all in a row.	5

Your task

Here are five explanations. Each one matches a line of the rhyme.

1. Read each explanation carefully then read the nursery rhyme again.
2. Put the line number next to the correct explanation.

The explanation	The line in the rhyme it fits
This line is about the fact that Queen Mary was supposed to have had some baby girls, who were born dead. She was supposed to have buried them in a long row.	
This line is accusing Mary of going against her father and brother just for the sake of it. She wanted to change England back from a Protestant country into a Catholic one.	
This line is laughing at Mary because she liked church bells ringing and music playing.	
This line is mocking Mary because she couldn't get pregnant. Nothing in her would grow.	
This line is about Mary's husband King Philip. He was always having affairs with other women. In those days, this was called cuckolding.	

16

☞

Your task ✎

Now you know what the rhyme really means, imagine you are the person who wrote it.

Draw a poster to go up on the walls of all the cities in England. Put the rhyme on it and add pictures to help people understand what it means.

What changes did the Tudor kings and queens make?

In the sixteenth century, the official religion of England was changed three times. This is what happened:

King Henry VIII ruled from 1509 to 1547. He was a Catholic but he made himself head of the Church of England instead of the Pope. The Church continued to be Catholic in every other way, although in his will Henry ordered that his son Edward should be brought up by Protestants.

King Edward VI ruled from 1547 to 1553. Edward was a very strict Protestant. He made sure that the Church of England became a Protestant Church. He died when he was only 16.

Queen Mary ruled from 1553 to 1558. She was the opposite of Edward. Mary was a very strict Catholic. She changed the official religion back to Catholic.

Queen Elizabeth I ruled from 1558 to 1603. Elizabeth was not a strict Catholic or a strict Protestant. However, she preferred the Protestants to the Catholics. So she changed the official religion back from Catholic to 'Church of England'!

Your task

Colour code the chart! Shade Protestant monarchs in orange and Catholic monarchs in green. Which monarch should be half green and half orange?

18

You will need
- pen or pencil
- coloured pencils

◆ **HISTORY DICTIONARY**

The important words	My explanation of them
minister	_____
Reformation	_____

How did changes in religion affect ordinary people?

In 1500, England had been a Catholic country.

By 1600, England was no longer a Catholic country. It was a Protestant country. There were no Catholic churches – only Protestant ones. There were no Catholic priests, only Protestant **ministers**.

All of these changes together were called the **Reformation**.

What had changed and what stayed the same?

Your task

1. Read through the information below. It tells you what changed and what stayed the same.
2. Underline all the changes in red.
3. Underline all the things which stayed the same in black.

People still went to church on Sundays.

However, Protestants did not believe in purgatory.

They did not believe you could pay to have your sins forgiven.

People still believed in the same God.

People still thought that you would go to heaven if you were good and to hell if you were bad.

People no longer had the 'last rites'.

People were still baptised.

People were still confirmed.

People still made marriage vows.

Catholics had liked highly decorated churches with lots of statues, paintings and ornaments, but Protestants preferred simple churches with plain walls.

They said services in English, not in Latin.

18

The inside of a Protestant church was very different from the inside of a Catholic church. Examine the two pictures on pages 3 and 4 carefully. Picture A is a Catholic church in 1500. Picture B is a Protestant church in 1600.

Your task A

Examine picture A.

1. Find the priest. Colour his vestments (his robes) in green.
2. Find the altar server. Colour his undergarment in black.
3. Find the two candlesticks. Colour them in yellow and gold.
4. Find all the angels and saints. Colour their haloes in yellow.
5. How many angels and saints are there? _____

Examine picture B.

1. Find the minister. Colour his robes in black. Leave his collar white.
2. Find the altar table. Colour it in brown.
3. Find the pulpit (where the minster went to give his sermon). Colour it in brown.
4. Leave the walls white and colour the floors in grey.

Your task B

1. What is your main impression of picture A?

_____

_____

2. What is your main impression of picture B?

_____

_____

3. If you were only allowed to use one sentence to describe the differences between the two pictures, what would it be?

_____

_____

Picture A

Picture A

Every time the official religion changed, the church had to change as well. These pictures show what happened at Melford church in Suffolk. However, they are in the wrong order! Can you decide on the correct order and draw a line from each caption to the right picture?

1548
Edward's reign

1555
Mary's reign

1562
Elizabeth's reign

19

You will need
- pen or pencil
- scissors

A Family Affair

Every time the official religion changed, the church buildings and church services had to change. This story tells you how these changes affected one priest and his family.

Your task

1. Read the story carefully.
2. This is a timeline of Uncle John's life. As you read through the story again, write down what happened to Uncle John on each of these dates. The first one has been done for you.

1509	Great-Uncle John was born
1527	
1547	
1553	
1600	

 What do you think might have happened to Ben and Emma after they were caught by the soldiers?

☞

Story

It was the year 1600. Emma and Ben were staying with their Great-Uncle John. He was the minister of the parish of Weaverham. One night, Uncle John told them about the old days.

'I am an old man now,' he said, '91 next birthday. I was born in 1509 when Henry VIII became king. Some people say I am the oldest man they have ever known. When I was young boy, England was a happy place to live.

'I became a Catholic priest and, in 1527, was given the parish of Melford. Then one day we heard rumours that King Henry had divorced his beautiful wife Catherine of Aragon and had married a six-fingered witch called Anne Boleyn.'

Great-Uncle John told Emma and Ben about the old days

Then he told them about King Henry's divorce

Emma and Ben looked shocked. Anne Boleyn was the mother of their Queen, Elizabeth. Surely the Queen was not a witch's daughter?

☞

'You are speaking treason, Great-Uncle John,' said Ben.

'I am an old man now. I am past caring what might happen to me,' Uncle John replied. 'In the past I tried to hide what I really felt, but I am Catholic and a Catholic I will stay. I don't like this Protestant Church of England.'

Ben and Emma looked at each other nervously. Great-Uncle John stared hard at them. 'Don't you see how silly all these changes are, children? I was a priest while King Henry was supporting the Pope. In 1547, when King Edward came to the throne, I became a Protestant minister. I became a priest again in 1553 when Mary became Queen. Now it is 1600 and I am supposed to be a minister because Queen Elizabeth has ordered it!'

Then Uncle John showed Ben and Emma a letter. It was addressed to the Minister at Weaverham. This is what it said:

We of the Catholic faith have heard that you prefer the old ways. On the third Sunday of next month, a Catholic priest will arrive in your parish. He will be staying at a secret place in the village.

If you wish, he will say the Catholic mass that evening. Are you willing to help us?

Uncle John looked at his great-niece and nephew.

Great-Uncle John showed Emma and Ben a letter in which he was told that a Catholic priest was coming to Weaverham to say mass

'I am going to let him come,' he said. 'I have made up my mind. I believe in the old Catholic ways. We can't use the church, of course, so I shall ask the priest to say mass in this house. Will you help me?'

Emma took Ben to one side so they could decide what to do. It did not take them long to make up their minds.

☞

'Uncle is 91 years old,' said Emma. 'We must help him.'

'The priest will do no harm,' said Ben. 'He is only going to say mass. He isn't plotting to kill the Queen or to force Protestants to become Catholics like Queen Mary did.'

'I agree with you,' said Emma.

They went back over to their great-uncle and told him they would do whatever they could to help.

'I knew I could trust you,' said Uncle John. 'Now, this is what we must do...'

The next day, Emma and Ben were taken into the church by their great-uncle. He unlocked a heavy wooden trap door just behind the altar and pointed to the wooden ladder inside.

'This is a secret passage,' he said. It leads down under the church and comes out at the river. A boat is moored there. Tell no one else about it.

Ben and Emma helped Great-Uncle John to get things ready for a Catholic mass

But right now I have another job for you. You must climb down the ladder and bring up the small chest which is hidden in the corner. It has got all the things that we need for a Catholic mass to be said.'

Soon it was Sunday and time to get the room ready for mass. Emma and Ben carefully laid out the altar cloth, candles and crucifixes.

Then there was a knock on the door. Ben ran to open it. There stood a strange man. He was quite young and very thin with a long beard.

'I am the priest; I've come to say mass,' he said. 'It is best if you don't know my name. Is everything prepared?'

He turned to their great-uncle.

'You must be the minister of Weaverham,' he said. 'It's very brave of you to have me here today. Have you some bread and ale for a starving priest?'

The Catholic priest arrived and Emma fetched him some food

They all laughed, and Emma was sent to fetch some food. As she entered the kitchen, she felt sure that a dark shadow had flitted past the window.

'It's just your imagination, girl,' she said to herself. 'Pull yourself together and get the meal for the priest.'

Ten minutes later, Emma was back in the dining room. Already there were five or six parishioners in there. Ben and Emma did not recognise anyone. Emma noticed that they were all quite old. No one seemed to have brought children.

After eating his meal, the priest moved quickly to the altar. He put on his robes and signalled to everyone to stand up.

☞

'*Pax vobiscum*,' he said.

Emma and Ben looked at each other.

'This must be Latin,' thought Emma. 'Nobody can understand what he is saying. I'm not sure that I like it all that much!'

Before she had time for another thought, the door behind her was flung open!

Queen Elizabeth's soldiers came to arrest the priest. Uncle John collapsed

'Halt in the name of Queen Elizabeth!' shouted a huge soldier. Two other soldiers rushed in behind him.

Everyone began to scream. The priest seemed to be fixed to the floor. Ben ran over to him and grabbed his shoulder.

'Quick, follow me,' he gasped. But the soldier had already seen the priest and was running towards them. Suddenly there was a loud crash.

'It's Uncle John... Somebody help him!' Emma screamed.

The soldier stopped in amazement and Emma turned on him.

'Look at what you've done,' she cried. 'You murderers!'

All the other people in the room took their chance and ran out as quickly as possible. Ben stopped only for a moment. He knew just what his uncle would have wanted him to do. Quick as a flash he grabbed the priest again and pulled him over to the window.

☞

'Over there, in the church,' Ben whispered. 'Just behind the altar there's a trap door. It leads to the river... a boat... quick, you must go!'

The priest tried to escape to the river, but the soldiers were waiting for him

The priest climbed out of the window and flew off. Ben turned to look at his sister. The soldiers turned to look at Ben.

'Well done, young man,' smirked the first soldier. 'So he's gone to the river, has he? Just as we hoped! Sergeant Beckworth is waiting for him. Then, of course, there's the rack, the thumbscrews and the burning coals. Which do you think your sister will like best?'

Ben ran to Emma. She was holding her poor uncle in her arms.

'Don't believe a word they say,' he shouted. 'Is Uncle all right?'

Emma burst into tears.

Your task

The soldiers have just burst in through the door. Write down what each of the people below would be thinking.

The Catholic priest

Great-Uncle John

The soldier

Emma

19

Your task A

Work in pairs.

1. Think of one important moment in the story. It can be any moment you like. You could choose the moment when Ben reads the letter. You could choose the moment when the soldiers arrive.
2. Write down what happened in your own words in **one** of the boxes on page 10.
3. See if you can fill the other boxes with other moments in the story.
4. When you have filled all five boxes, cut out each box carefully. Give the five slips of paper to your partner.
5. See if your partner can put **your** parts of the story in the right order. (You have to do the same with your partner's five slips of paper!)

Did everyone in your class choose the same moments in the story to write about? If some people chose different parts of the story, what does this tell you about how history is recorded?

Your task B

1. Read the story again.
2. Make a list of those people who could have betrayed the Catholic priest.
3. Explain why you think they might have wanted to betray him.

People who might have betrayed the Catholic priest	Reasons why they might have wanted to betray him
_____	_____
_____	_____
_____	_____

4. Discuss your list with a friend.
5. Decide between you who was the most likely person to have betrayed the priest.
6. Write your conclusions down below.

We think the priest was probably betrayed by

_____

_____

Record one moment of the story in each box, then carefully
cut out the boxes.

20

You will need
- pen or pencil
- dice
- counters

♦ **HISTORY DICTIONARY**

The important words	My explanation of them
Puritan	

Who were the Puritans?

As you have already discovered, there were many changes in religion between 1500 and 1600. Despite this, there was a group of people who felt that the changes did not go far enough. Although they were members of the Church of England (Protestants), they were known as **Puritans** because they wanted to clean (purify) the Church of all the bad things that **they** believed were still happening in it.

Puritans hated Catholics. They felt that the Catholic Church was more interested in making money than in helping people. They hated the Latin services which no one could understand. They hated the statues and decorations in Catholic churches because these statues seemed to be more important to Catholics than God himself.

Puritans liked plain churches without statues or pictures on the walls. They liked ministers to wear plain clothes. They liked simple services said in English. They believed that you should work hard. They also believed that Sunday was the most important day of the week. On this day people should give themselves entirely to God.

In the seventeenth century, the Puritans became more and more powerful. They probably changed the way that people in England worshipped and thought more than any of the Tudor kings and queens did.

Your task

1. There are ten pictures and ten captions on pages 3, 4 and 5.
2. Write the correct caption under each picture.
3. Decide which column on page 2 each of the pictures and captions belongs in.
4. Write the captions in the correct columns on page 2.

Write the captions in the correct column.

Things the Puritans say you must do on Sundays	Things the Puritans say you must not do on Sundays

Match these pictures with the captions on page 5 and write the correct caption under each column.

Match these pictures with the captions on page 5 and write the correct caption under each column.

Match these captions with the pictures on pages 3 and 4.

You must not be lazy	You must read the Bible
You must not go dancing	You must visit your sick friends and relatives
As the sun rises, you must kneel and pray	You must not go drinking and feasting
You must not play cards	You must not work in the fields
You must go to church and listen to the sermons	You must give bread and water to poor people

Darkness and light

The Puritans called the set of things they approved of the 'works of light' and the set of things they did not approve of the 'works of darkness'. The lists you made on page 2 show some of the things the Puritans liked, and some of the things they did not like. Here are some more:

The Puritans approved of	The Puritans did not approve of
simple clothes saving money plain, white churches simple furniture services in English working hard discussing religion with your friends being honest children obeying parents	Catholic statues or paintings in churches lying going to the theatre music in church gambling going to brothels swearing horse racing cockfighting bull baiting or bear baiting

Your task

You are going to make up your own snakes and ladders game.

1. Choose some actions the Puritans would have approved of.
2. Draw some ladders on your board and write these actions at the tops of the ladders. (Remember – the better and holier the action, the longer the ladder should be!)
3. Choose some actions the Puritans would have disapproved of.
4. Draw some snakes and put these actions at the bottoms of the snakes. (The really wicked actions should have longer snakes.)

When you have finished making your game, play it with your friends.

Works of Darkness and Works of Light

FINISH

START

THE MAKING OF THE UK SUPPORT MATERIALS

21

You will need

- pen or pencil

Why did England become a Protestant country?

Ernest Muddle has got into a terrible mess. He has been given ten reasons why people in England became Protestants and he can't work out which are correct. You now know a lot about the subject. Can you help him?

Your task

1. Cross out the incorrect reasons.
2. Write the correct reasons in Ernest's think bubbles on page 2.

■ People in England thought that the Catholic Church was too rich.

■ Everybody in England hated Italians.

■ People in England thought that the Catholic priests and bishops were lazy.

■ People in England preferred the name Protestant to Catholic.

■ People in England didn't like draughty churches.

■ People in England didn't like the mass being said in Latin.

■ People in England had to follow the official religion of their country.

■ People in England preferred Protestant hymns to Catholic hymns.

■ People in England wanted to be different from everybody else.

21

22

Were the Catholics framed?

Queen Elizabeth never married. She had no children. So when she died in 1603, Elizabeth's cousin James became the next king of England. He was already King James VI of Scotland. In 1603, he became King James I of England as well. This was the end of the **Tudor** dynasty and the beginning of the **Stuart** dynasty.

Your task

You are going to complete the family tree on the next page. Some of it has been done for you. The rest of monarchs are below. Draw them in the correct places.

Henry VIII 1509–1547

Charles I 1625–1649

Elizabeth I 1558–1603

Edward VI 1547–1553

Charles II 1660–1685

Mary I 1553–1558

Henry VII
1485–1509

The Tudor family tree

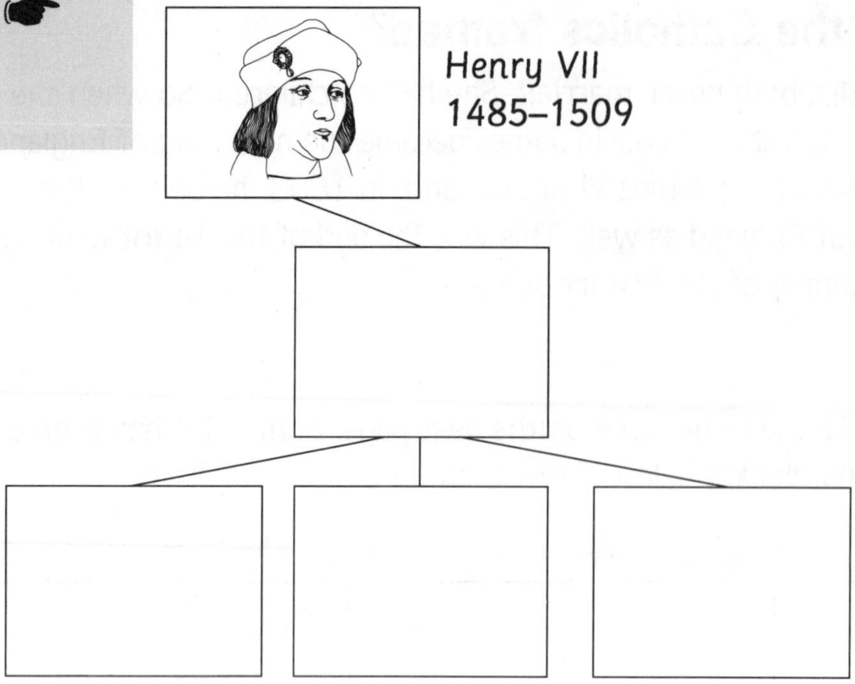

James I
1603–1625

The Stuart family tree

James II
1685–1688

Mary, who married
William of Orange
1689–1702

Anne
1702–1714

King James and the Catholics

King James had a chief adviser called Robert Cecil. He hated Catholics.

Your task

1. Read this story. It is from a children's history book. It was written in 1835.
2. Draw in the missing parts of the story.

King James dealt severely with the Catholics. He put many of them in prison and took a lot of money from them.

The Catholics grew tired of this. Some of them thought that if they could kill him, they might have a Catholic king or queen.

From thinking wickedly they went on to do wickedly. They found that there were some cellars under the Houses of Parliament and they filled these cellars with gunpowder.

They hired a man called Guy Fawkes to set fire to the gunpowder and to kill the members of Parliament and the King on November 5th.

One of the lords, whose name was Mounteagle, had a friend amongst the Catholics, and that friend wrote him a letter without signing his name.

He begged him not to go to Parliament that day because a sudden blow would be struck that would destroy them all.

Lord Mounteagle took this letter to the King's Council. The King thought about it and said the sudden blow must mean gunpowder.

He set people to watch the cellars under the Parliament, till at last they caught Guy Fawkes with his lantern, waiting for the time to set fire to the gunpowder.

3. Whose side do you think the author was on, the Catholics' or the King's?

_____

4. Write down the clue in the story which helped you to decide the answer.

_____

_____

_____

22

Were the Catholics framed? Using the evidence

Some people do not accept this story. They say that Robert Cecil, who was King James's chief adviser, planned the whole thing. They say that Cecil hoped this would make King James punish the Catholics and that he would learn to hate all Catholics.

Some people say that one of the supposed plotters, a man called Francis Tresham, was actually working for Robert Cecil. They say that it was Tresham who sent the anonymous letter to Mounteagle and that the Catholics were 'framed'!

Your task

Examine the following sources very carefully. Each source will give you evidence about the Gunpowder Plot. When you have studied each piece of evidence you must come to your own conclusions.

You must decide which of these two statements is correct:

1. The Catholics were framed by Robert Cecil because he hated them and wanted King James to hate them.

2. The Catholics had a very clever plot to kill the King and blow up Parliament. It was just good luck that the government found out about the plot in time to stop it.

Good luck!

SOURCE 1 This picture of the Gunpowder plotters was made by a Dutch artist. He had probably never seen the plotters. He was probably a Protestant

1. How has the artist made the men look sly and secretive?

_____

_____

☞

2. Read this source. It was written by an Italian Catholic. According to him, this is what Robert Cecil said.

SOURCE 2 Written by the ambassador from Venice

We cannot hope for good government while we have a large number of people who obey foreign rulers as the Catholics do. The priests preach that Catholics must even kill the King to help their religion.

3. What problems were the Catholics causing for Robert Cecil?

_____

_____

_____

_____

4. Read Source 3. It is part of the letter sent to Lord Mounteagle. The messenger was disguised. Lord Mounteagle got the letter on October 26th. It was the only night in 1605 that he stayed at home.

SOURCE 3 From the letter sent to Lord Mounteagle

My Lord. I have a care for your safety. Make up some excuse to miss Parliament. Go into the country because something dreadful is going to happen.

5. Why do you think the messenger was in disguise?

_____

_____

_____

_____

☞

6. Look at Source 4. Why do you think Guy Fawkes' signature on the confession is so different from his normal signature?

_____

_____

_____

SOURCE 4 Guy Fawkes' normal signature next to his signature to his confession

7. Does this mean that Guy Fawkes' confession could not be trusted?

_____

_____

8. Read Source 5 and underline all the sentences in this source that make you think that Robert Cecil **had** 'framed' the Catholics.

SOURCE 5 Some important facts to consider

The 36 barrels of gunpowder were put in the cellar of a house next to Parliament. This house was rented to the plotters by a friend of Robert Cecil.

Lord Mounteagle told the King about the plot on October 27th and yet the government didn't do anything until November 5th.

The government seemed to know where all the plotters were. On November 7th they were captured. Even though they did not try to escape, some of them were shot dead.

The only plotter to be set free was Francis Tresham. He was recaptured when the trial of the other plotters was over. He died of a mysterious illness in the Tower of London on December 23rd 1605.

◆◆◆◆◆◆◆◆◆◆◆◆◆◆◆◆◆◆◆◆◆◆◆◆◆◆◆◆◆◆◆

9. You have examined a lot of sources. You have considered the facts. What conclusions have you reached? Complete your final report.

My conclusions about the Gunpowder Plot

From the evidence I have received I am of the firm opinion that the correct

statement (from page 5) is _____

_____

_____

_____

_____

_____

The reasons **why** I have come to this judgement are

1. _____

2. _____

3. _____

4. _____

5. _____

6. _____

Signed _____
History Detective

23

There are two pages to this task

◆◆◆◆◆◆◆◆◆◆◆◆◆◆◆◆◆◆◆◆◆◆◆◆

You will need
- pen or pencil

◆ **HISTORY DICTIONARY**

The important words	My explanation of them
civil war	_____

Why did civil war break out in 1642?

After Guy Fawkes was executed for treason in 1605, King James ruled the country for the next twenty years.

When King James died in 1625, his son Charles became King of England. Over the next few years, King Charles ran into trouble. By 1642 England was divided by a civil war.

By 1645, Charles had lost the war, but things got worse for him. In 1649, he was executed!

Some people say that Charles made a lot of wrong decisions and this is why he lost the war and was eventually executed. Would **you** have made the same decisions if you had been Charles?

Your task

You are going to play a game called 'The King's Choices'. The board is on page 2.

The game is for two to four players. You are candidates for the kingship. Each of you has to make decisions about what to do. The person who makes the most sensible decisions becomes king, takes Charles's place and changes the face of history!

How to play

1. One person in the group reads out event number 1.
2. He/she reads out the two options that are available.
3. The group discusses each option.
4. Individuals in the group decide which option **they** would take.
5. Record **your** decision on the score card your teacher will give you.
6. Move on to event number 2.
7. Continue until you have made decisions about all eleven events.

At the end of the game, your teacher will give you the answer sheet. Count up your marks. The person with the **lowest** score is the winner!

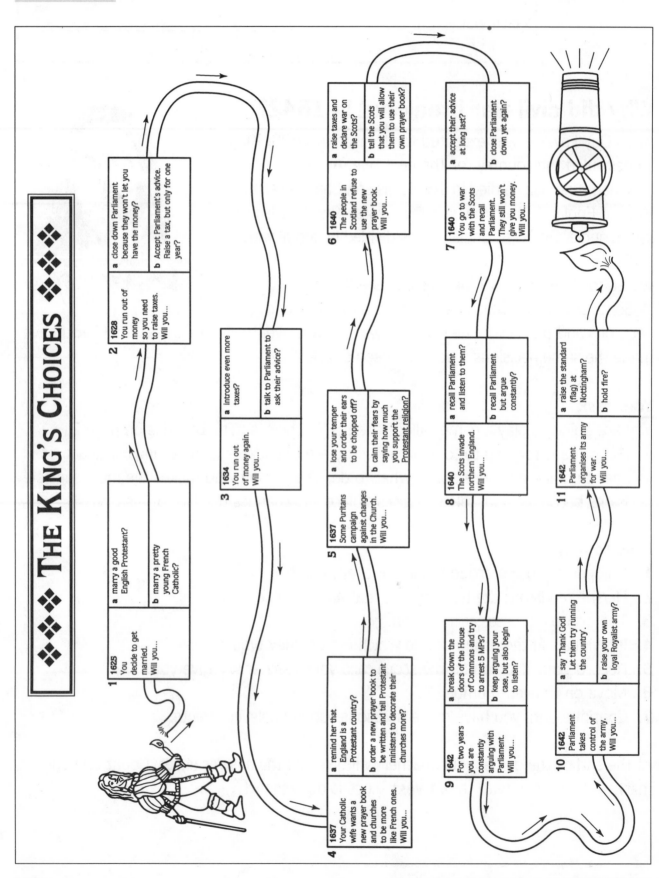

❖❖❖ THE KING'S CHOICES ❖❖❖

1 1625
You decide to get married. Will you...
- **a** marry a good English Protestant?
- **b** marry a pretty young French Catholic?

2 1628
You run out of money so you need to raise taxes. Will you...
- **a** close down Parliament because they won't let you have the money?
- **b** Accept Parliament's advice. Raise a tax, but only for one year?

3 1634
You run out of money again. Will you...
- **a** introduce even more taxes?
- **b** talk to Parliament to ask their advice?

4 1637
Your Catholic wife wants a new prayer book and churches to be more like French ones. Will you...
- **a** remind her that England is a Protestant country?
- **b** order a new prayer book to be written and tell Protestant ministers to decorate their churches more?

5 1637
Some Puritans campaign against changes in the Church. Will you...
- **a** lose your temper and order their ears to be chopped off?
- **b** calm their fears by saying how much you support the Protestant religion?

6 1640
The people in Scotland refuse to use the new prayer book. Will you...
- **a** raise taxes and declare war on the Scots?
- **b** tell the Scots that you will allow them to use their own prayer book?

7 1640
You go to war with the Scots and recall Parliament. They still won't give you money. Will you...
- **a** accept their advice at long last?
- **b** close Parliament down yet again?

8 1640
The Scots invade northern England. Will you...
- **a** recall Parliament and listen to them?
- **b** recall Parliament but argue constantly?

9 1642
For two years you are constantly arguing with Parliament. Will you...
- **a** break down the doors of the House of Commons and try to arrest 5 MPs?
- **b** keep arguing your case, but also begin to listen?

10 1642
Parliament takes control of the army. Will you...
- **a** say 'Thank God! Let them try running the country'.
- **b** raise your own loyal Royalist army?

11 1642
Parliament organises its army for war. Will you...
- **a** raise the standard (flag) at Nottingham?
- **b** hold fire?

ANSWERS

Event 1 A= 0 B=10
Event 2 A=10 B= 0
Event 3 A=10 B= 0
Event 4 A= 0 B=10
Event 5 A=10 B= 0
Event 6 A=10 B= 0
Event 7 A= 0 B=10
Event 8 A= 0 B=10
Event 9 A=10 B= 0
Event 10 A= 0 B= 0
Event 11 A=10 B= 0

YOUR SCORE

Over 100

You are completely unsuited to kingship. You are hasty and thoughtless. If only you had made one or two different decisions, the English Civil War would never have happened.

Between 50 and 100

You haven't done too badly. Although you are rather tyrannical, the people will tolerate you because they believe so strongly in the monarchy. At least the chances of there being a civil war are quite remote.

Less than 50

If only you had been king instead of Charles. None of this would have happened. The country would have been governed properly and the monarchy would have gone from strength to strength. You probably would have had many more children so that the Stuart kings and queens would still be with us today!

Score card

Name _____

Event number	A or B?	Score

Total score _____

You will need

- pen or pencil
- coloured pencils

◆ **HISTORY DICTIONARY**

The important words	**My explanation of them**
Parliamentarian	_____
Royalist	_____
siege	_____

What was life like during the Civil War?

Civil wars are terrible things. People have to take sides. Often friends, neighbours and family members take different sides. They are forced to fight one another even if all they want is peace.

This happened during the English Civil War. Some people supported Parliament. They were called **Parliamentarians**. Others supported the King. They were called **Royalists**. People on both sides had their homes burned down. Men, women and children were killed. Sometimes whole villages were destroyed.

Your task

Divide into pairs. One of you is a Royalist, the other a Parliamentarian.

1. Each of you should design a poster with words and drawings showing how terrible the other side's soldiers are. Use the information from these sources to help you.
2. Then compare your drawings.

SOURCE 1 A description of what soldiers did during the Civil War

They ran into every house, cursing and damning, threatening and terrifying poor women most terribly, setting naked swords and pistols to their breasts. They were picking purses and pockets, searching in holes and corners for money or goods. In every street they made fires with gunpowder, wisps of straw, hay and burning coals.

SOURCE 2 Parliamentary soldiers in a church

SOURCE 3 A print published during the war showing Royalist soldiers

S in C pp. 52–55   *THE MAKING OF THE UK SUPPORT MATERIALS*

A case study: Lady Harley defends her castle

During the Civil War, people did things that they would never normally have done. Do you think that a woman would be strong enough to guard her home against 700 armed troops?

Brilliana, Lady Harley, was a Puritan. She supported Parliament. She lived at Brampton Castle in Herefordshire. The castle was attacked by the Royalist soldiers. They were led by a man called William Vavasour. The **siege** lasted from July 1643 to January 1644. It ended when Lady Harley caught a chill and died.

Your task

Work in pairs.

Read the letters your teacher will give you. Some were written by Lady Harley and some by William Vavasour. Unfortunately Ernest Muddle has mixed the letters up and even lost all the signatures.

1. Sort out those which you think were written by Lady Harley and those which were written by William Vavasour.
2. Put them into chronological order.
3. Add the correct signature to each letter.
4. Use the evidence from these letters to write your own account of the siege of Brampton Castle.

 Do you think that Lady Harley was brave or foolish to oppose the Royalists for so long?

Account of the dreadful siege of Brampton Castle, written by

_____

The castle was owned by_____

She was a _____

In July 1643 it was attacked by _____

They were led by a man called _____

These are some of the things that happened during the siege: _____

_____

_____

_____

_____

_____

_____

_____

_____

_____

_____

_____

Photocopy these letters, cut them out and shuffle them.

26 July 1643

*There are troops and horses facing our castle. There are at least 700 of them.
We have only 50 musketeers inside the castle.*

Signed

26 July 1643

*I summon the honourable and valiant Lady Harley to surrender the castle. We
wish to prevent further inconvenience to her.*

Signed

26 July 1643

*I dare not, I cannot, I must not. I have the law of nature, of reason and of the
land on my side. The castle belongs to my husband.*

Signed

26 July 1643

If you refuse, you will suffer. The soldiers will attack your friends and family.

Signed

27 July

My dearest son,
They have stolen all the cattle from outside the castle walls. My life and the
lives of my little children are in danger.

Signed

31 July

If you lay down your arms, we will guarantee safety for you and
your children.

Signed

August

My soldiers are angry. I cannot stop them from using rotten language that
infects the air. They are calling everyone inside the castle Harley's bastards, as
well as rogues and thieves.

Signed

August 1643

They have shot at us, burned the parsonage and barns down and nearly
destroyed our west wall. Some soldiers are even firing at us from the
church steeple.

Signed

✂

August 1643

The King has written to me. He thinks I have had bad advice. I wrote back and told him that the castle belongs to my husband by the law of the land.

Signed

August 1643

If you surrender, I will give you and your servants a free pass to march safely away.

Signed

September 1643

I took no notice of him and ordered my musketeers to shoot at them. This has taught him a lesson. They are bloody villains.

Signed

9 September 1643

The Lord was this day pleased to take away these bloody villains. Our food has nearly run out and the roof of the castle is battered, but we have driven them away.

Signed

24 September 1643

My dear son,
I am worried that the troops will come back. This time they will take no notice
of the fact that I am a woman. I am frightened that we will all be killed.

Signed

9 October 1643

I have taken a great cold. It is an ill time to be sick. But I look death in the
face without dread.

Signed

October 1643

Now that Lady Harley has died you will see the good sense of surrender.

Signed

January 1645

It has taken you six months to come to your senses. But I will be kind to you.
If you go at once to the Governor of Ludlow Castle, he will look after you and
Lady Harley's children, Tom, Ned, Dorothy and Margaret. Brampton Castle
now belongs to the Royalists.

Signed

25

There are three pages to this task

◆◆◆◆◆◆◆◆◆◆◆◆◆◆◆◆◆◆◆◆◆◆◆◆◆◆◆◆◆◆

You will need

- pen or pencil

◆ HISTORY DICTIONARY

The important words	My explanation of them
treason	_____
dock	_____
	_____

Why did the English execute their king?

King Charles and his Royalist army lost the Civil War. Two years later he fought another civil war against Parliament. Charles lost again.

Parliament decided that the King had to be put on trial for **treason**. The date was set for January 20th 1649. The trial was to take place in Westminster Hall. But on the first day, many people who were supposed to be there to judge the King failed to turn up! In fact, only 68 people out of 135 were there. They were probably too scared to send a king to his death.

Source 1 is a description of King Charles's trial.

SOURCE 1 Written by a modern historian

At one end of the hall were the benches for the judges.

In the middle, raised above everyone else a little, was John Bradshaw, the President.

Down either side of the hall were lines of soldiers.

*Opposite the judges was a **dock** – with a crimson chair facing the judges.*

Around the top were galleries for the more important spectators.

Your task

Source 2 on the next page is a picture of King Charles's trial. The historian who wrote Source 1 used it to help him describe what happened.

1. Match each sentence in Source 1 to the correct part of the picture and write it in the box provided. (The first one has been done for you.)

SOURCE 2 The trial of King Charles

At one end of the hall were the benches for the judges.

2. Read Source 3. It tells you what King Charles looked like on the first day of his trial. It also tells you how he acted.
   a) Underline the words and phrases which show that the author liked King Charles.
   b) Below the source write your account of the trial. Imagine you dislike King Charles. The first few lines have been written for you.

SOURCE 3 Written by a supporter of the King

He was a small man who walked with short steps. He was dressed entirely in black. His beard was tinged with grey and it was less finely trimmed than it had been. His hair fell down to his shoulders and was still thick, though it was streaked with grey. Those who had not seen him since the Civil War would have noticed the sunken eyes and the pouches beneath them. He looked like a man who had suffered. It was the face of one who had fought hard and perhaps knew he had lost. Yet there was a maturity in the face. Nor was it a face of an old and sick man, and when he spoke, people noticed his stammer had gone.

Your account as an opponent of the King

He was small and weedy. He could hardly walk properly. He looked like the devil,

dressed all in black. _____

_____

_____

_____

_____

_____

_____

_____

_____

26

You will need
• pen or pencil

The Trial of King Charles I – a play

This is a modern play, but the writer has used a lot of the words spoken at the original trial in January 1649.

Characters

Narrator
John Bradshaw – President of the Court
Simon Moore – The Clerk to the Court
King Charles
Caroline Sweet – First spectator
Jane Davis – Second spectator
Gerald Baxter – Parliamentarian soldier
Francis Hale – Parliamentarian soldier
Veronica Maunders – Servant at Carisbrooke Castle

Non-speaking parts

Two guards
Up to twelve judges
Several soldiers
Several spectators

Act One. Scene 1. Westminster Hall.

The First Day: Saturday January 20th 1649
Everyone files slowly into the room

Clerk to the Court	Will you all take your seats please. Soldiers down both sides of the hall. Spectators at the far end. Quickly now. Make way for John Bradshaw, the President of the Court, and the rest of the judges.
John Bradshaw	*(striding through)* You're doing a fine job, my friend. Today is the most important day in the history of England. Today a king is to be tried for treason. In 300 years' time, people will read about this day and will praise us for what we have done.
Narrator	Everyone took their rightful places and then silence fell. The story began in 1642, when King Charles and his Royalist army went to war with the Parliamentarian army. The Royalists lost the war and King Charles was sent to prison in Carisbrooke Castle. He started plotting with the Scots and tried to persuade them to invade England. There was a second civil war which the King also lost. Now it is January 1649, and King Charles is being tried for treason.

◆━◆━◆━◆━◆━◆━◆━◆━◆━◆━◆━◆━◆━◆━◆━◆━◆━◆━◆

Clerk to the Court	Bring the prisoner to the dock. *(Two guards appear, one on either side of the King.* *Slowly they lead him to the dock)*
Caroline Sweet	*(Leans over to her friend)* Just look at him. He's so thin and grey.
Jane Davis	Serves him right! All the pain and torment he's caused us. I've lost my husband and two sons thanks to this war.
Caroline Sweet	I know, but after all he is our King. He looks like a man who has suffered, doesn't he? Just look at his eyes. They look lost. I think he knows what is going to happen to him.
Jane Davis	A fair trial and a fair result. That's what will happen to him. He'll go to the block and none deserves it more than him!
Clerk to the Court	Silence in court.
Narrator	Everyone turned to look at President Bradshaw. He had a piece of paper in his hand. He looked straight at King Charles and began to read:
John Bradshaw	Charles Stuart, King of England, Scotland and Wales, trusted to use your power for the good of the people; you stand accused of overthrowing the rights and freedom of the people, taking away the power of Parliament, and making war against Parliament and the people. How do you plead? Innocent or guilty?
King Charles	I refuse to answer to these charges. Neither you *(pointing at Bradshaw)* nor anyone else in this room has any legal right to put me on trial.
Narrator	After this, there was an uproar. Spectators started shouting and Bradshaw turned to consult the judges on either side of him. Eventually the Clerk to the Court spoke.
Clerk to the Court	I call this session to an end. We will meet again on Monday at the same time.

◆◆◆◆◆◆◆◆◆◆◆◆◆◆◆◆◆◆◆◆◆◆◆◆◆◆◆◆◆◆◆◆◆◆◆

Scene 2. Westminster Hall.

The Second Day: Monday January 22nd 1649

Narrator

The day began just as Saturday had, with Bradshaw speaking. King Charles was even more angry.

John Bradshaw

Charles Stuart, you are guilty of all the treasons, murders, burnings, damages and mischiefs to this nation committed in the wars.
How do you plead?

King Charles

Parliament is not a court of law.

John Bradshaw

Confess or deny the charge.

King Charles

By what authority do you sit?

Narrator

Take him away.
(The two guards lead the King out of the courtroom)

Scene 3. Westminster Hall.

Witnesses are called

Narrator

The same thing happened on the third day of the trial. After this, the judges banned Charles from coming to the court.
They began calling witnesses to accuse Charles of various crimes.

Clerk to the Court

I call Gerald Baxter to bear witness to the court.

John Bradshaw

And what have you got to say?

Gerald Baxter

(stammering) I was there, Sir, on that dreadful day in August 1642.
King Charles, Sir, he was dead set on war.
We tried to stop him but he wouldn't listen.
He raised his standard at Nottingham and started the whole sorry business.

◆◆◆◆◆◆◆◆◆◆◆◆◆◆◆◆◆◆◆◆◆◆◆◆◆◆◆◆◆◆

John Bradshaw	Thank you for your honourable testimony. Now who have we next? Ah yes, Francis Hale. What have you got to tell us? *(Francis Hale is led forward)*
Francis Hale	I started the war siding with the King, your Honour. But then I got sickened by the way he treated prisoners after we'd captured Leicester. Why, I swear by God's own holy breath that he said 'I do not care if they cut them three times more, for they are mine enemies!'
Narrator	There were horrified murmurs from the spectators. Even Bradshaw looked shocked. The Clerk to the Court called the final witness.
Clerk to the Court	I call the final witness for the prosecution. Veronica Maunders.
Veronica Maunders	*(producing a crumpled piece of paper in her hand)* Your 'ighness, I swear I am only a poor servant at Carisbrooke Castle but I knows an evil man when I sees one! When Charles was prisoner in the castle, he asked me to deliver this letter secretly. I knew it was wrong. Not that I can read, you understand. But I took it straight to my husband who told me to take it to the Justice.
Narrator	The letter was read out to the court. It showed that while Charles had supposedly been trying to make peace with Parliament, he was secretly asking his son to raise another army to fight again.

☞

Scene 4. Westminster Hall.

Verdict and sentence: Saturday January 27th 1649

Narrator

On January 27th, the court sat again and Charles was brought before the judges for the verdict and sentence. Charles was promised he could make a speech before the verdict was read out.

King Charles

Mr. President, I want to talk to my people. Let me speak to the House of Commons and the House of Lords. I have a plan for peace.

John Bradshaw

You had time enough to speak to the Commons and Lords before the war. But you chose to close Parliament down. I forbid you to speak to them now.

King Charles

If you won't let me speak to the Commons and the Lords, at least let me speak to all the people gathered in here.

John Bradshaw

You refused to answer our charges at the beginning of the trial. You have lost your opportunity now. It is too late. This is the sentence that the court has passed upon you. Charles Stuart, King of England, Scotland and Wales, you are guilty of failing in your duty to see that parliaments were called. You have attacked the basic liberties of this country.
Therefore... this court does judge that Charles Stuart, a tyrant, traitor, murderer and public enemy of the people, shall be put to death by the severing of his head from his body.
(There is a huge gasp from the people in the courtroom, then a deathly hush)

Narrator

The execution was fixed for January 30th.
The death warrant still had to be signed. In the end less than half of the original 132 judges signed it. The others refused.

☞

Act Two. Scene 1. The Scaffold at Whitehall.

(Crowds are milling around the scaffold, where there is an axeman's block and two guards, one with an axe in his hand)

Narrator

On the morning of January 30th Charles rose early. He asked for two shirts since it was cold and he did not want to appear to be shivering from fear. He was then taken to Whitehall, where he ate a piece of bread and drank some wine and then prayed.
At two o'clock he stepped on to the scaffold.

(King Charles is led into the room. He walks up to the block, kneels down and the executioner slowly raises his axe. As the axe falls [careful here!] the crowd groans, cries, moans and shouts. They all rush forward to surround the body)

Narrator

The souvenir hunters rushed to dip their handkerchiefs in the dead king's blood and to take hairs from his head and beard.
Then the soldiers came charging in to force the crowd to leave.
Everyone ran for their lives.

The next day, King Charles's head was sewn back on to his body.
A few days later, the body was quietly buried at Windsor Castle.

◆▬◆▬◆▬◆▬◆▬◆▬◆▬◆▬◆▬◆▬◆▬◆▬◆▬◆▬◆

Your task

Imagine you are King Charles. It is the night before you are due to be executed. What will your thoughts be?

I was King of England for nearly 25 years. During

that time I tried to _____

_____

My poor son Charles will never be king now because

_____

_____

The thing that frightens me most is _____

_____

Supposing the axe is blunt. Then _____

_____

But I must not show I am scared. I will _____

_____

Dear God,

Here is my final prayer: _____

_____

27

You will need
- pen or pencil
- paper
- scissors
- glue
- source sheets

◆ **HISTORY DICTIONARY**

The important words	My explanation of them
republic	_____
Lord Protector	_____
rebellion	_____

What kind of man was Oliver Cromwell?

After King Charles was beheaded, England had no king or queen. A country which is governed without a king is called a **republic**.

After a few years, in 1653, Oliver Cromwell became ruler of the country. He had been an important General in Parliament's army He was now known as **Lord Protector**.

Historians have tried to decide what kind of man he really was. What sort of man would see his king beheaded and then take over the government of the country himself?

To help you to answer these questions, you will need to ask two other questions first:

1. What did Oliver Cromwell do when he was ruler of the country?
2. Why did he do these things?

27

What did Cromwell do?

Your task

1. Read the story of Oliver Cromwell.
2. Underline all the dates and what happened on them.
3. Make a timeline of these events.
   (You can choose what sort of timeline you want to make.)

The story of Oliver Cromwell, 1649–60

In 1649, Oliver Cromwell had to go to Ireland where there was a **rebellion**. Cromwell's army defeated the Irish.

When Cromwell got back from Ireland, he tried to make Parliament pass new laws. Parliament kept holding up these new laws. This made Cromwell so angry that he closed Parliament down. This was in 1653.

Then, in the same year, Cromwell set up a new parliament. It decided to make him more powerful. He was given the name Lord Protector.

In 1654, another new parliament argued with Cromwell about religion. He did not like this. So, in 1655, he closed this parliament down too.

By 1657 the country was in a mess. There were riots and complaints about high taxes. Some people said that Oliver Cromwell should become king. They said that this would solve all their problems.

Cromwell turned down the offer, but he did accept a new law which said that his son Richard would become Lord Protector after he died, in just the same way as a king would pass on his crown to his son.

On September 3rd 1658, Oliver Cromwell died. His son Richard took over. By May 1659, Richard decided it was too difficult to run the country. He resigned his job and went back to being a farmer.

Finally, in 1660, Parliament, the army and the people invited Charles Stuart, son of the executed King Charles I, to return as king. He accepted, and England had a monarchy again.

 Were Oliver Cromwell's actions really any different from those of King Charles?

27

Why did Oliver Cromwell do what he did?

Historians still disagree about why Cromwell acted as he did.

- Some say he was trying to grab power for himself.
- Some say he just wanted to find a better way of governing the country.
- Some say he believed in giving the people greater freedom.
- Some say he crushed anyone who disagreed with him.

Use the evidence to decide for yourself!

Your task

1. Write each of these four headings on a separate sheet of paper.

a) **Oliver Cromwell was trying to grab power for himself**
b) **Oliver Cromwell wanted to find a better way of governing**
c) **Oliver Cromwell believed in giving people greater freedom**
d) **Oliver Cromwell crushed anyone who disagreed with him**

2. Take one source at a time from the sets of sources and explanations your teacher will give you.
3. Read each source carefully, and match it with the explanation of what it means.
4. Talk about the source in your group and decide which of the four statements it proves.
5. Place the source and the explanation on the correct sheet of paper. (You may think it proves more than one statement, in which case you will have to ask your teacher for a second copy to stick on another sheet.)
6. When you have discussed all the sources and placed them all on the correct pieces of paper, check with your teacher and then glue them down.

 Using the information you have just analysed, decide why Oliver Cromwell acted as he did.

SOURCE 1 Cromwell's letter to the House of Commons, 17 September 1649

Our army came to Drogheda (in Ireland) on September 3rd. On Tuesday 10th after some hot fighting, we entered. Our men were ordered by me to put all to the sword. I also forbade them to spare any people in the town who had weapons.

In the great church almost 1000 of them were put to the sword, fleeing there for safety. This is the righteous judgement of God upon those barbarous wretches who have dipped their hands in so much innocent blood. It will help prevent bloodshed for the future.

EXPLANATION A

Cromwell never wanted to be leader of the country. He only did it because he thought the country would fall apart otherwise.

SOURCE 2 An eye-witness account of Cromwell in Parliament

Lord General Cromwell came to the House. After a while he got up. He spoke of the good things that Parliament had done. Then he began pacing the floor and said, 'You are no Parliament, I say you are no Parliament; I will end your sitting.'

Then he said to Colonel Harrison, 'Call them in,' and twenty or thirty musketeers entered. Then Cromwell, pointing to the Speaker, said to Harrison, 'Fetch him down'.

EXPLANATION B

Most people in the army thought that Cromwell shouldn't call himself king. They said it would be going against God. They said King Charles's son Charles Stuart might come back again.

SOURCE 3 Written by Bishop Burnet 50 years after the events

Cromwell would rather have taken a shepherd's staff than the Protectorship. Nothing went more against his feelings than a show of greatness. But he saw it was necessary at the time to keep the nation from falling into extreme disorder.

EXPLANATION C

Cromwell wanted people to see him exactly as he was.

SOURCE 4 From Clarendon's *History of the Rebellion*

This man, against the desires of all noble persons, took the throne of three kingdoms. Without the name of king, but with a greater power and authority than had been claimed by any king.

EXPLANATION D

This source tells you that Oliver Cromwell went to Ireland. He and his soldiers were fighting the Irish. Cromwell was winning. So nearly 1000 people ran into a church for safety. Cromwell ordered his men to kill everyone in the church. He said it would stop even more bloodshed later on.

SOURCE 5 From a diary reporting a meeting between Cromwell and army officers

One hundred officers said to Cromwell that he should not take the title of King because it was not pleasing to his army. It was a matter of scandal to the people of God, it was dangerous to his person and it would make way for Charles Stuart to come in again.

EXPLANATION E

Cromwell did not agree with what people in Parliament were saying. He called in 20 or 30 soldiers and arrested the Speaker (the person in charge).

SOURCE 6 A copy of a picture of Cromwell, painted in 1650. He told the artist, *'Paint my picture exactly like me, and do not flatter me at all, but show all these wrinkles, pimples, warts and everything as you see me.'*

EXPLANATION F
Cromwell tried to bribe the army officers so that they would support him in his plans to become king.

SOURCE 7 From the memoirs of Edmund Ludlow, written at the time

Cromwell tried all possible means to persuade the army officers to approve his plan (to become king). He invited himself to dine with General Fleetwood and Colonel Desborough, where he began to go on about the monarchy. They told him that those who offered it were friends of Charles Stuart.

EXPLANATION G
Cromwell ruled over three kingdoms even though he was never called king. He had more power than any king had ever had before.

SOURCE 8 Description of Cromwell's crowning as Lord Protector, June 1657

As he entered Westminster Hall, His Highness was dressed in a robe of purple velvet lined with ermine, being the dress used in the investiture of princes.

EXPLANATION H
When Cromwell was crowned as Lord Protector, he dressed himself to look like a king.

28

You will need
- pen or pencil

◆ **HISTORY DICTIONARY**

The important words	**My explanation of them**
Bill of Mortality	_____
	_____

How did the Great Plague affect the City of London?

Do you remember learning about the Black Death? This was a plague which swept right across Asia, India and Europe during the 1340s and 50s. People got huge boils under their arms and in their groins. Most people who caught it died.

Over the next 300 years, plagues similar to the Black Death kept returning to Britain. In 1665, one of the worst ever epidemics broke out. In London itself, 80,000 people died.

The problem was that people still did not know what caused plague and disease. Even though 300 years had passed, it was as if time had stood still as far as finding the causes of and cures for the plague were concerned!

Your task

Examine Source 1 (on page 2) very carefully. It is a copy of the **Bill of Mortality** (list of deaths) for one week in London in 1665.

1. How many people died in this week? (You could use a calculator to help you to answer this question.)

_____

2. Which were the three most common causes of death?

_____

_____

_____

SOURCE 1 The Bill of Mortality for one week in London, 1665

Abortive	6	Gangrene	1	Scowring	13
Aged	54	Gowt	1	Scurvy	1
Apoplexie	1	Grief	1	Sore legge	1
Bedridden	1	Griping in the Guts	74	Spotted Feaver and Purples	190
Cancer	2	Jaundies	3	Starved at Nurse	1
Childbed	23	Imposthume	18	Stilborn	8
Chrisomes	15	Infants	21	Stone	2
Collick	1	Killed by a fall down stairs at St. Thomas Apostle	1	Stopping of the stomach	16
Consumption	174	Kingsevil	10	Strangury	1
Convulsion	88	Lethargy	1	Suddenly	1
Dropsie	40	Murthered at Stepney	1	Surfeit	87
Drownd two, one at St.Kath. Tower, and one at Lambeth	2	Palsie	2	Teeth	113
Feaver	353	Plague	3880	Thrush	3
Fistula	1	Plurisie	1	Tissick	6
Flox and Small-pox	10	Quinsie	6	Ulcer	2
Flux	2	Rickets	23	Vomiting	7
Found dead in the Street at St.Bartholomew the Less	1	Rising of the Lights	19	Winde	8
Frighted	1	Rupture	2	Wormes	18
		Sciatica	1		

28

☞

3. Choose four diseases from Source 1.
a) Write their names in the boxes below.
b) Find out what they were. Your teacher will be able to help you.
c) Draw a picture of what you think they looked like.

Name of disease	Name of disease	Name of disease	Name of disease
What it means	What it means	What it means	What it means
What it looked like	What it looked like	What it looked like	What it looked like

◆-◆

Source 2 describes one person's view of what life was like in London during the plague of 1665. It was written by Samuel Pepys. He was living in London at the time.

Your task 📖 ✎

1. Read what he had to say about the plague.
2. Underline all the sentences which describe how Pepys tried to avoid catching the plague.
3. Underline all the sentences which describe how other people tried to avoid catching the plague.

SOURCE 2 Extracts from Samuel Pepys' diary, 1665

7 June *This day I did in Drury Lane see two or three houses marked with a red cross upon the doors and 'Lord Have Mercy Upon Us' writ there. This worried me so much that I bought a roll of tobacco to smell and chew.*

29 June *Travelled by water to Whitehall, where the court was full of wagons and people ready to go out of town.*

20 July *I hear the sickness is scattered almost everywhere. My Lady Carteret did give me a bottle of plague water.*

12 August *My Lord Mayor commands people to be inside by nine at night that the sick may leave their homes for air and exercise.*

3 September *Dare not wear my new periwig, bought in Westminster where the Plague is. Nobody will dare buy any hair for fear of infection, that it had been cut off the heads of people dead from the Plague.*

---

4. Which, if any, of these ways to avoid catching the plague would have been successful?

_____

_____

5. How do we know that Samuel Pepys had no real idea of what caused the plague?

_____

_____

_____

29

There are six pages to this task

You will need

- pen or pencil
- scissors
- glue
- sheets of paper

How do we know about the Great Plague?

One of the best ways to find out about the plague is to read Samuel Pepys' diaries. You have already read some of his work. However, his diaries are very long.

Another excellent way of finding out about the plague is to look at some of the 'plague broadsheets' which were written and drawn at the time. These were just like our newspapers and comics today. They kept people informed about what was going on, and what steps were being taken to prevent the plague from spreading.

Your task

1. Cut out the pictures and written descriptions on pages 2–5.
2. Match each written description to the correct picture.
3. Put the pictures and descriptions in the correct order.
4. Glue them on to a large sheet of paper to make your own broadsheet.

Cut these out and match each one with the correct description.

John Dunstall fecit.

Cut these out and match each one with the correct description. ✂

Cut these out and match each one with the correct description.

THE MAKING OF THE UK SUPPORT MATERIALS

☛

◆◆◆◆◆◆◆◆◆◆◆◆◆◆◆◆◆◆◆◆◆◆◆◆◆◆◆◆◆

Cut these out and match each one with the correct picture. ✂

The first shows the nature of the disease, which was vomiting, and the sick lying in their beds, one laid out ready to be put into the coffin. Others are recovered and, being lame by reason of their sores, walk with staves (sticks) about the room.

The second was the manner of shutting up the houses with a watchman, a red cross and 'Lord have mercy upon us' on the door. There are searchers with white sticks in their hands, dog killers killing the dogs, also the fires that were made in the streets, and the sedan (a closed chair, carried by two people) carrying the sick to the pesthouse.

The third shows many people escaping from London by water in boats and barges loaded with goods.

The fourth shows them escaping by land on horseback, in coaches and in wagons with their goods, the country people stopping them to see their certificates.

The fifth shows the manner of carrying the bodies to be buried by the bearers with red staves in their hands, so that people know they should keep away from them. Some bearers ring a bell.

The sixth shows that in some places the dead were carried in carts to be buried, and also birds falling dead to the ground.

The seventh shows the manner of burying the dead.

The eighth shows the manner of burying the dead with their friends accompanying them.

The ninth shows their return to the city.

Your task

1. Look at picture 2 and its description. Make a list of all the ways that were used to try and stop the plague from spreading.

_____

_____

_____

2. Look at pictures 3 and 4 and their descriptions. How did the people of London try to get away from the plague?

_____

_____

_____

3. Look at picture 5 and its description. Why would the coffin carriers hold a red stick in their hands?

_____

_____

_____

4. Look at pictures 7, 8 and 9 and their descriptions. Explain in your own words how plague victims were buried.

_____

_____

_____

30

You will need

• a role card

Plague comes to Eyam – September 1665

To start with, it was just the people of London who were affected by the plague. But people knew that the plague could easily spread to their own village or town.

In the village of Eyam, a tiny place in the hills of Derbyshire, a tailor called George Vicars arrived home with a bale of cloth from London. The cloth was rather damp and smelly after the long journey, so he spread it out near to the fire and tried to dry it all out. Then he went across the street to visit Mary Walters. He had a letter for her from his old friend Matthew Fullerton.

Matthew had been living for the past ten years in East Cheap in London. He was a tailor, just like his friend George. He wrote to Mary asking if he could stay with her and her widowed mother whilst the plague raged in London. Matthew assured Mary that he had a certificate from the East Cheap Authorities saying that he was clear of the plague.

Mary was very worried about this letter. She was not sure whether it was 'proper' to have Matthew staying with her. She was worried about the threat of plague, since he lived in London. So Mary went to see the Vicar, a man called William Mompesson. He suggested they should have a meeting of the whole village to discuss the issue.

Everyone in the class will be at the meeting. Some will support the idea of Matthew coming. Some will be against the idea.

◆◆◆◆◆◆◆◆◆◆◆◆◆◆◆◆◆◆◆◆◆◆◆◆◆◆◆◆◆◆◆

Your task 📝 💬

You are going to be one of the villagers at the meeting.

You will be given your name and a description of yourself.

You will be told whether you have to support the idea of Matthew coming to the village, or oppose it.

You will also be given some ideas about what arguments to use.

But you must find some other arguments too.

■ You could use your History textbooks.

■ You could do some research in the library.

■ You could refer back to the work you did on the Black Death, since attitudes hadn't changed much!

The characters

(Several of these were real people)

Mary Walters – spinster (an unmarried woman)

Joan Walters – cloth worker

John Sheldon – squire (an important landowner)

Elizabeth Sheldon – the squire's wife

Margaret Blackwell – servant to the squire's wife

Marshall Howe – sexton (church organiser and caretaker)

Martha Howe – the sexton's wife

Bertha Shakeshaft – midwife

Rowland Mower – cooper (a barrel maker)

Andrew Merrill – hermit

George Vicars – tailor

William Mompesson – vicar

George Saville – Earl of Devonshire

Henrietta Bradshaw – widow

Richard Talbot – blacksmith

Catherine Talbot – the blacksmith's wife

Matthew Mortin – farmer

Maria Mortin – farmer's wife

John Hancock – farmer

Elizabeth Hancock – farmer's wife

Your name is: Mary Walters

You are 28 years old and unmarried. Your father died when you were six years old and you have lived alone with your mother ever since. You spin wool which your mother weaves into cloth. You dislike your mother and are scared of her.

You **want** Matthew Fullerton to come to the village because:

1. There is a chance that he might ask you to marry him.
2. It is good to have a man about the house.
3. Matthew is hard-working and he could carry on his trade as a tailor in the village.
4. The plague is unlikely to affect a strong, healthy man like Matthew. Anyway, he has a plague certificate.
5. If the vicar gives his blessing, then there is nothing to worry about.

(Now add any other arguments you would like to put forward.)

Your name is: Joan Walters

You are 50 years old and your husband died when you were 28. You live in a small cottage with your daughter Mary. You dislike Mary, blaming her for all your bad luck. You rely on her to spin the wool for your cloth and, in fact, she is the only person in the village who takes much notice of you. She has to!

You **don't want** Matthew Fullerton to come to the village because:

1. You are selfish and you want Mary to stay with you because you can boss her about.
2. If Mary got married, there would be no-one to spin wool for you.
3. As Mary's husband, Matthew would take over the cottage and perhaps try to throw you out.
4. There must be something wrong with him; no one in his right mind would want to marry Mary.
5. He went off to London to seek his fame and fortune. Now he is coming back with his 'tail between his legs'. Why should you have to look after him?

(Now add any other arguments you would like to put forward.)

Your name is: John Sheldon

You are 45 years old, married with four children. As local squire you have numerous servants, gardeners and attendants. You are reasonably popular with the villagers because you are fair and considerate when it comes to collecting taxes and sorting out petty legal arguments.

You **want** Matthew Fullerton to come to the village because:

1. He is a strong, healthy young man who will be useful to you.
2. He is a tailor by trade and the village is short of such men. You hope that he and George Vicars will work in partnership together.
3. Matthew will bring new blood into the village. Perhaps he will marry Mary and they will have children who in later years will bring further prosperity to the village.
4. The plague couldn't possibly come to Eyam. The village is far too clean, prosperous and well-run, thanks to your organisation.

(Now add any other arguments you would like to put forward.)

Your name is: Elizabeth Sheldon

You are the squire's wife. You are timid and God-fearing. You love your husband a great deal, even though you think he can be rather boring at times. You are fond of entertainment, music and dancing and are particularly keen on the young men who visit your home to give lessons to your children.

You **want** Matthew Fullerton to come to the village because:

1. Your husband wants him to come, and you always agree with him.
2. He seems a nice, harmless young man.
3. You know that plague is always carried by bad smells and you intend to carry your pomander around with you all the time.
4. Mary needs a husband. You don't like her mother Joan and wish to see a little happiness enter Mary's life.

(Now add any other arguments you would like to put forward.)

✂

Your name is: Margaret Blackwell

You are a lively, cheerful young girl. You are 17 years old and have been a servant up at the manor house for the past six years. You work hard for the squire and his family but enjoy having the occasional evening out with your friends.

You **want** Matthew Fullerton to come to the village because:

1. He is a bachelor with a respectable trade. You are young and pretty. He might want to marry you.
2. If Matthew became interested in you, you could get your own back on Mary. You don't much like her because she disapproves of you enjoying yourself and frequently makes unkind remarks about you.
3. Matthew is young and fit like you. People who are young and healthy just don't get plague. Only the old, smelly, dirty and mean people get it; people like Mary's mother.

(Now add any other arguments you would like to put forward.)

Your name is: Marshall Howe

You are 40 years old, married to Martha and have three young children. As the sexton, you make sure all the villagers attend church regularly and chase up all those who fail to pay their 'Poor Rate'. You are a busybody and like to interfere in people's affairs. Most people dislike you and suspect that you keep some of the church takings for yourself.

You **don't want** Matthew Fullerton to come to the village because:

1. Eyam is a very superior village and you don't want any 'cheap jack' from London bringing unpleasant habits into the village.
2. You have heard that Matthew is rather fond of drink.
3. If the villagers allow Matthew in, then people from all over the country will want to come and stay.
4. He might already be carrying the plague. In fact it is highly likely, given the sort of characters he hangs around with.

(Now add any other arguments you would like to put forward.)

Your name is: Martha Howe

You are 38 years old, married to Marshall the sexton, and have three young children. You are proud to be the wife of such an important person and, being the village gossip, are delighted with the opportunities it gives you to know everyone's business.

You **don't want** Matthew Fullerton to come to the village because:

1. Your three young children will be at risk of getting the plague.
2. You've heard scandalous rumours about Matthew's drinking problems. Apparently he likes to flirt with women too.
3. You always agree with what Marshall thinks. Just as every good wife should.

(Now add any other arguments you would like to put forward.)

Your name is: Bertha Shakeshaft

You are an elderly midwife who has spent all her life in the village. In fact, you were present at Mary's birth and have taken a keen interest in her welfare ever since. Your herbal remedies are renowned and when you were younger you were able to perform quite complicated surgery.

You **want** Matthew Fullerton to come to the village because:

1. It is about time Mary had a husband.
2. Mary is a good woman who will be able to have lots of strong, healthy children which you will deliver.
3. Your herbal remedies are excellent. Even if Matthew does fall ill, you are confident that your infusion of willow bark will cure all the plague symptoms.

(Now add any other arguments you would like to put forward.)

Your name is: Rowland Mower

You are 30 years old and a bachelor. You have lived alone since your mother died six months ago. You are a cooper by trade but can turn your hand to all sorts of odd jobs. You have recently begun to notice how pleasant Mary is looking. You think about her when you are alone in your house with no one to cook or clean for you.

You **don't want** Matthew Fullerton to come to the village because:

1. He was a rival of yours when you were much younger and you never liked him.
2. Mary is too good for the likes of Matthew Fullerton. She shouldn't have to look outside the village for companionship.
3. Although Matthew hasn't got the plague, he might bring his three dogs with him. Everyone knows that they carry plague.

(Now add any other arguments you would like to put forward.)

Your name is: Andrew Merrill

You are a hermit. You live alone in the woods with only your cat and the birds for company. You talk to yourself a great deal and are frequently seen singing and chanting. You like boiling leaves, plants and grubs for your food. You are harmless but very scatty.

You **want** Matthew Fullerton to come to the village because:

1. Your motto is 'Live and let live'.
2. The talk of plague is all nonsense. You have consulted the stars and there is nothing in them that makes you think plague is near.
3. Your potions are very effective as magical remedies against the plague. In fact they are much more effective than those herbal remedies suggested by Bertha the midwife.

(Now add any other arguments you would like to put forward.)

Your name is: George Vicars

You are a middle-aged bachelor and have spent all your life in Eyam. You lodge with the Widow Cooper and her two sons in a cottage just a stone's throw from the church. As village tailor, you think you are superior to other folk in the village. You are often lonely because you have very few friends.

You **want** Matthew Fullerton to come to the village because:

1. He is obviously a 'good sort'. In fact, he has just given you a parcel of the best woollen cloth from London which is hanging in front of the fire to dry out.
2. With two tailors in the district, you will be able to offer a quality service and expand your business into neighbouring villages.
3. Matthew is in serious danger of being infected with plague whilst he is living in London. As Christians, we should be doing our best to rescue him from danger.

(Now add any other arguments you would like to put forward.)

Your name is: William Mompesson

You live and work in Eyam with your wife and two children. You have been vicar in the village for two years and are getting a reputation for hard work and sincerity. Mary is particularly fond of you and frequently visits you to talk over her problems.

You **want** Matthew Fullerton to come to the village because:

1. Mary truly loves him and love conquers all. She might be able to stop him drinking.
2. The rumours about his drink problems are only based on hearsay. There is no proof. The villagers ought to give him a chance to prove his worth.
3. God will protect the people of Eyam from the plague because they are good, clean-living folk.
4. Even if Matthew has sinned by going away to London, he is like the prodigal son who should be welcomed back into the fold.

(Now add any other arguments you would like to put forward.)

Your name is: Sir George Saville, Earl of Devonshire

You are 65 years old and the most important person in the whole of Derbyshire. You are a cousin to John and have been staying at the manor house with the Sheldon family. Your own home is at Chatsworth House and the purpose of your visit is to persuade John to finance a trading partnership you want to establish with a merchant in Genoa in order to set up your younger son in business.

You **don't want** Matthew Fullerton to come to the village because:

1. In your travels you have come across plague victims and the sight of their terrible suffering has affected you badly.
2. In your travels you heard rumours that plague can be passed on by poisonous air. Matthew might bring some of these smells into the village on his clothing.
3. You have heard that Matthew is a womaniser. As an upstanding lord you can't allow that sort of fellow near the good folk of Eyam.

(Now add any other arguments you would like to put forward.)

Your name is: Henrietta Bradshaw

Your are a wealthy widow whose husband died in 1646. You don't much care about village affairs and are in fact planning to go and live with your daughter Ann in Treeton.

You **want** Matthew Fullerton to come to the village because:

1. When he was a little boy, he was very kind to you and ran errands for you whilst you were caring for your sick husband.
2. Matthew could perhaps live in the servants' quarters of your house and make sure the house is kept in order until you can find someone to buy it.
3. Plague is only spreading in London and the big cities. It is over forty years since the last epidemic. You don't think that a tiny village like Eyam could possibly be affected.

(Now add any other arguments you would like to put forward.)

Your name is: Richard Talbot

You are the village blacksmith working at Riley Forge. You are an honest, God-fearing man and spend all your spare time either in church or in the company of your wife and six beloved children. You are very proud of your three sons and three daughters.

You **don't want** Matthew Fullerton to come to the village because:

1. Although you realise his reputation as a 'drinker' is only rumour and gossip, you wish to protect your wife and children from the slightest hint of scandal.

2. Matthew might have a plague certificate, but if plague is raging in London, he could have caught it **since** the certificate was issued.

3. If the villagers allow Matthew in, then other 'undesirables' might follow.

(Now add any other arguments you would like to put forward.)

Your name is: Catherine Talbot

You are Richard the blacksmith's wife. You are a quiet, unassuming woman. You spend all your time looking after your six children. The eldest child is preparing to visit relatives in far-off Lancashire, so you are busy making him new clothes and sorting out his belongings.

You **don't want** Matthew Fullerton to come to the village because:

1. You find it difficult talking to strangers, and although Matthew isn't quite a stranger, he has probably been 'tainted' with London ways and manners.

2. Although **you** don't agree with gossip, nevertheless these rumours about Matthew being a drinker are very worrying. Supposing he becomes a bad influence on your children, or even on your husband?

3. Even if Matthew doesn't bring plague, he could bring other diseases such as the pox, or scrofula or dysentery. You don't want your children to be exposed to such a risk.

(Now add other arguments you would like to put forward.)

Your name is: Matthew Mortin

You are a 35-year-old farmer struggling to make a living on a small farm at 'Shepherd's Flat', an area on the outskirts of the village. Your wife is expecting your fourth child who will join Matthew aged 5, Robert 3, and Sarah 2.

You **don't want** Matthew Fullerton to come to the village because:

1. Even if he hasn't got plague, your wife is in a delicate condition and any extra worries could badly affect her health.
2. The village has limited resources and Matthew has a large appetite. It will be difficult to find enough food for him.
3. Supposing Matthew does get the plague. Who will look after him? Bertha the midwife is needed for your wife. You don't want her attention going elsewhere.

(Now add any other arguments you would like to put forward.)

Your name is: Maria Mortin

You are 33 years old, happily married to Matthew, who is a farmer, and expecting your fourth child. You live and work on the farm with your particular responsibility being the chickens, goats, pigs and the vegetable garden.

You **don't want** Matthew Fullerton to come to the village because:

1. There is no physician within miles of Eyam. You rely entirely on Bertha and your own herbal remedies from the garden. If Matthew comes and does get the plague, there could be huge problems.
2. George Vicars has served the needs of the village more than adequately over the past ten years. Why should the village have to put up with a second, unnecessary tailor?
3. Nobody is really sure how plague is spread. Matthew might bring the plague with him on the clothes he is wearing.

(Now add any other arguments you would like to put forward.)

Your name is: John Hancock

You are a 50-year-old farmer and the long-suffering husband of your gossipy wife Elizabeth. You work hard to provide for your children and love your wife dearly despite her faults. However, you try not to get involved in her petty quarrels.

You **want** Matthew Fullerton to come to the village because:

1. You wouldn't dare oppose your wife.
2. You think all these rumours about the plague being so bad are exaggerated. You've had boils before and they always clear up if you chew on a rind of bacon.
3. You can't really see what all the fuss is about. Plenty of people come in and out of the village. Any one of them might be carrying the plague.

(Now add any other arguments you would like put forward.)

Your name is: Elizabeth Hancock

You are 45 years old and have six children: John, Elizabeth, William, Oner, Alice and baby Ann. Your husband John is a farmer. Your farm is situated close to the blacksmith's forge and you have developed an intense hatred of the Talbots. The trouble is, Catherine Talbot seems unaware of your venom. This makes you even more angry and determined to be unpleasant.

You **want** Matthew Fullerton to come to the village because:

1. Catherine Talbot, the blacksmith's wife, **doesn't** want him to come.
2. You are keen to witness the quarrel that is bound to erupt between Margaret Blackwell and Mary Walters as they fight for his favours.
3. You don't think George Vicars is a particularly good tailor and Matthew might be able to teach him a thing or two.

(Now add any other arguments you would like to put forward.)

31

You will need

• pen or pencil

How did London change?

The Great Fire of London, 1666

The event which changed London more than anything else was the Great Fire. It began on September 2nd 1666 and destroyed nearly all the city.

■ 13,000 houses were burned down

■ 87 children died in the fire

■ Nearly a hundred churches and many workplaces were destroyed.

When the people began to rebuild the city, they used a different style of building and different materials.

Your task

On page 2 there are drawings of houses built before and after the Great Fire.

1. On Source 1, label everything that you think would help the fire to spread. One example has been done for you.

2. Label everything on Source 2 which made the houses less likely to catch fire.

3. Why do you think the people of London decided to make these changes?

_____

_____

_____

_____

_____

4. Why do you think they hadn't made these changes **before** the Great Fire?

_____

_____

_____

_____

_____

SOURCE 1 Before the fire. Label everything that you think would help the fire to spread

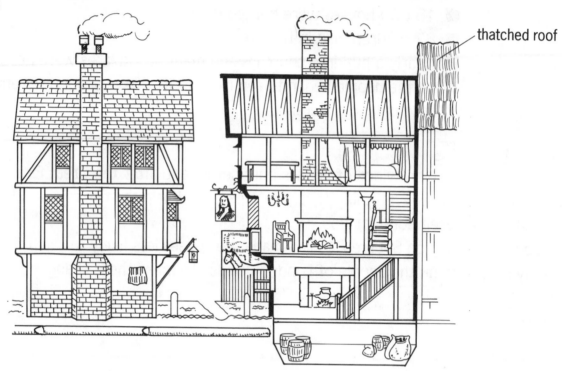

thatched roof

SOURCE 2 After the fire. Label everything which made the houses less likely to catch fire

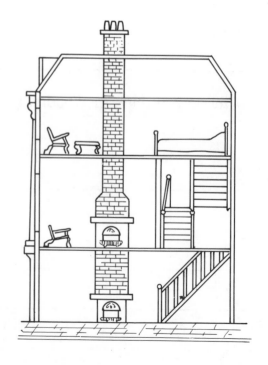

32

The story of the Great Fire of London

The Great Fire began in a bakery in Pudding Lane. It lasted for nearly a week. It burned down most of the city of London.

The bakery was owned by a man called Thomas Farynor. He was the King's baker. He had a daughter called Hannah.

Hannah was always being asked to tell people what really happened during the week of the fire. Sometimes, as she got older, she found it hard to remember everything. But she still enjoyed telling the story.

Your task

You are going to see whether Hannah is remembering things correctly by comparing her story with other sources of evidence.

1. Read Hannah's story on the next five pages.
2. Alongside each part of the story is another source. Underline or circle those parts of the sources which match Hannah's story.
3. Use Sources 5 and 7 to write the missing parts of Hannah's story.

Hannah's story

I still remember that dreadful night on Sunday September 2nd, when my father's bakery in Pudding Lane caught fire. We were woken in the middle of the night and could hear the fire crackling up the wooden stairs. We couldn't get down the stairs. We had to run up to the attic and climb out of the window on to the roof.

SOURCE 1 From Samuel Pepys' diary, Sunday September 2nd 1666

Jane called us up about 3 in the morning to tell us of a great fire they saw in the city. So I rose and went to her window. . . I thought it far enough off, and so went to bed again to sleep.

Father shouted at me to jump across from our roof to the house opposite. It was quite easy because all the houses were so closely packed together.

SOURCE 2 Buildings in London before the fire

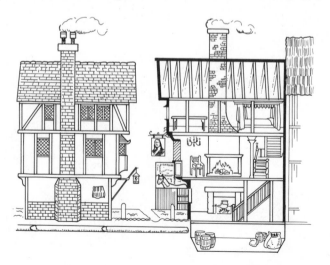

Hannah's story

The bakery worker who had first smelled the fire jumped across first. Then I jumped. But the maidservant just screamed and screamed and ran back inside. Father tried his best to stop her, but in the end he had to jump to safety. Poor Meg, she died in the fire.

SOURCE 3 From a school history textbook

Farynor's terrified maidservant was too scared to follow Farynor and the others on to the roof and so perished in the burning house. The Great Fire of London had claimed its first victim.

By the time morning came, everyone in the street had escaped into Thames Street. You could see the river from there. We all thought we would be safe if we stood on London Bridge.

SOURCE 4 Map showing the area where the Fire started

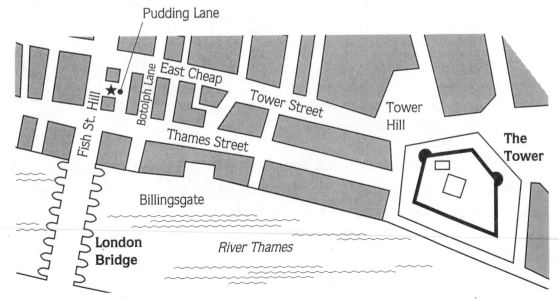

Hannah's story

SOURCE 5 From John Evelyn's diary, Monday September 3rd 1666

God grant my eyes may never behold the like, who now saw above ten thousand houses all in one flame, the noise and crackling, the shrieking of women and children, the hurry of people, the fall of towers, houses and churches, and the air so hot and inflamed that, at the last, no one was able to approach it.

By Monday, the fire had spread so far that King Charles and his brother, the Duke of York, were blowing up houses with gunpowder. I think they did this because if the houses weren't there, the fire would not spread from one house to another. But it didn't work!

SOURCE 6 From John Evelyn's diary

The King and the Duke of York rode up and down giving orders for blowing up houses with gunpowder. . . and standing still to see these orders obeyed, they exposed themselves to the very flames and ruins of the buildings ready to fall on them.

Hannah's story

SOURCE 7 St Paul's Cathedral in flames

Etiam periere Ruinæ

SOURCE 8 From Samuel Pepys' diary, Friday September 6th 1666

Walked thence and saw all the town burned, and a miserable sight of St Paul's church, with all the roofs fallen.

☞

Hannah's story

London was such a sad, sad sight after the fire. It changed completely. All the timber-framed houses were burned. Churches, prisons and warehouses. . . they all disappeared.

I remember being very upset and wondering what would happen to me and my father, and if anyone would remember poor Meg, our servant.

SOURCE 9 Lady Hobart writing from her home in Chancery Lane, Tuesday September 4th 1666

I am sorry to be the messenger of such dismal news, for poor London is almost burnt down. There never was so sad a sight, my heart is not able to express the thousandth part of it.

Your task

1. Make a list of all the different types of evidence which you have compared with Hannah's story.

The evidence which I have used:

_____

_____

_____

_____

_____

2. Look at Picture Source 13a, which also shows the Great Fire. Discuss with your friends and your teacher whether this gives you any new or different evidence.

33

You will need
- pen or pencil

The London coffee houses

Another big change which took place in London in the seventeenth century was the way in which people started visiting coffee houses rather than pubs and taverns. The first coffee house in London was built in 1652 by a man called Pasqua Rosee. Soon there were dozens of coffee houses all over the city. You might not think this sounds very important – but read through this information and see if you change your mind.

Why did people go to coffee houses?

1. People went to coffee houses to drink coffee and to smoke tobacco. These were new products which had been brought back to England from America. One hundred years earlier no one had heard of them. Now everyone wanted to drink coffee and smoke tobacco.

3. People came to talk business. London was growing in importance as the business centre of England. Many people made deals with customers at the coffee houses.

2. People also went to coffee houses to talk politics. Many of the coffee houses became the headquarters of a political party. Now that Parliament had much more say in running the country, political parties had become more important as well.

4. People came to exchange news. The first newspapers were just appearing. Newspapers would be read and discussed at the coffee houses and people would be able to find out what was happening elsewhere in the country much more quickly than they had in earlier centuries.

33

page 2

◆◇◆◇◆◇◆◇◆◇◆◇◆◇◆◇◆◇◆◇◆◇◆◇◆

☞

Your task

1. Look carefully at the outline drawing on page 3. It is a copy of a painting made in 1668. Find these things in the picture and write in the correct numbers:

■ a woman being given cups to wash ☐

■ a waiter putting clay pipes in a box ☐

■ a big pot of coffee being boiled on an open fire ☐

■ a waiter pouring coffee for two gentlemen ☐

■ two men looking at a painting by candlelight ☐

■ groups of men chatting and reading newspapers. ☐

2. Read Source 1. It was written in 1700 by a man called Ned Ward. He was describing a coffee house that he had visited.
3. Underline all the descriptions in the written source that match what you can see in the picture on page 3.

SOURCE 1 Written by Ned Ward in 1700

There was a rabble reminding me of a swarm of rats in a cheese store. Some came, others went; some were scribbling, others were talking; some were drinking coffee, some were smoking and some were arguing. . . There were clay jugs, long clay pipes, a little fire in the hearth, and over it a huge coffee pot.

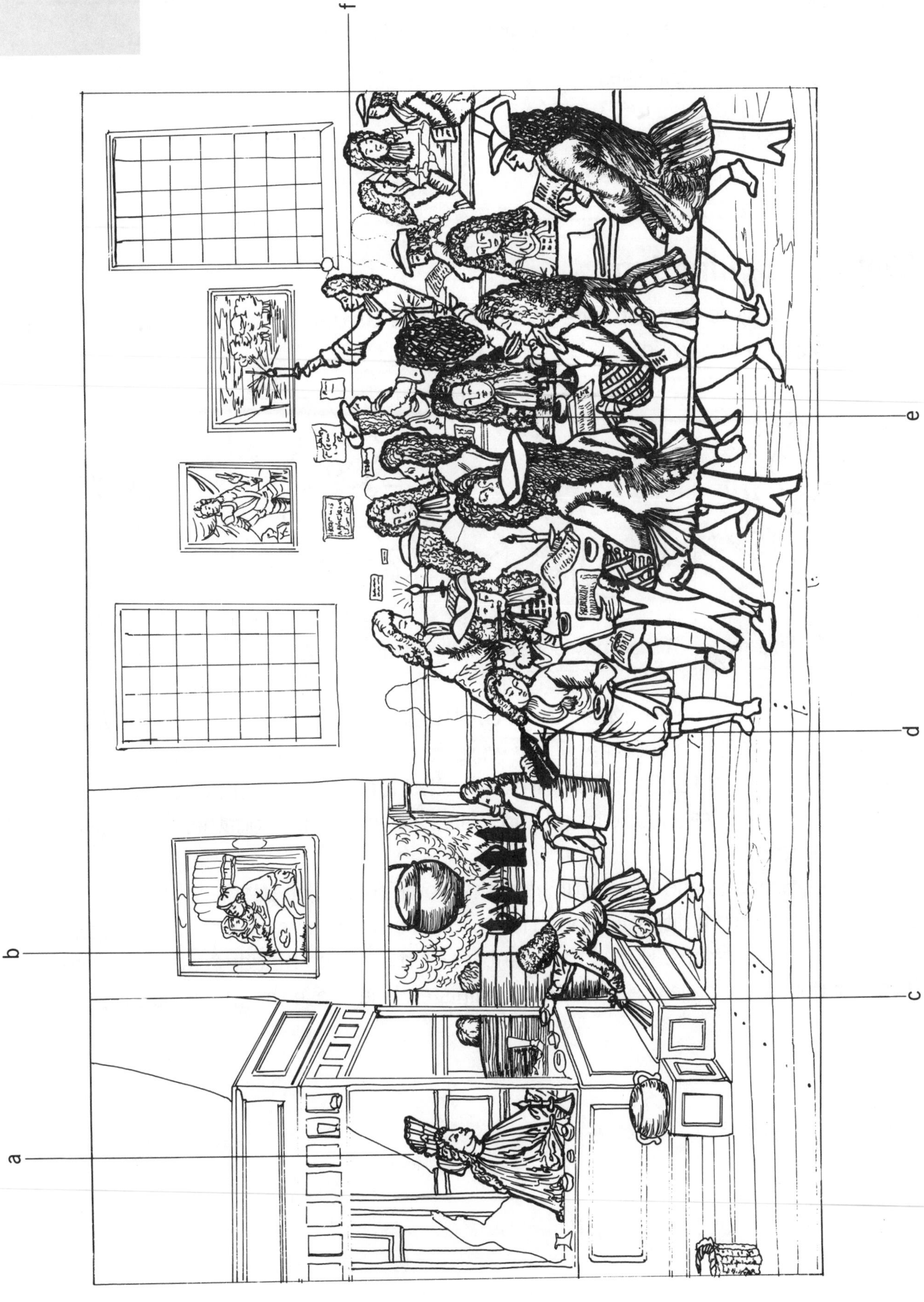
a
b
c
d
e
f

34

You will need
- pen or pencil

♦ **HISTORY DICTIONARY**

The important words	My explanation of them
British Isles	_____
nation	_____
United Kingdom	_____

Uniting the kingdom

In 1500 there were four separate countries in the **British Isles**. Each **nation** had its own special sign or symbol:

| A rose for England | A shamrock for Ireland | A daffodil for Wales | A thistle for Scotland |

By 1750, they were no longer separate countries. England, most of Ireland, Wales and Scotland were all joined together. They were ruled by the government in London.

Nowadays, in the 1990s, part of Ireland called Eire is a separate country. England, Northern Ireland, Scotland and Wales are still joined together and called the **United Kingdom**.

England, Scotland and Wales still have their own flags. The people who live there still think they come from different countries. Each country has its own football, netball, hockey and rugby teams. But all the countries of the United Kingdom are governed from London. They have the same Prime Minister. They have the Queen as their ruler.

Your task 🔍 🖊

On pages 3–5 there are three maps of the British Isles.

The first map shows you what the British Isles looked like in 1500.

The second map shows you what the British Isles looked like in 1750.

The third map shows you what the British Isles look like now.

On the map on page 3 the artist has drawn the symbols for each different nation.

1. Put the correct names of the countries in the empty boxes.

2. How has the artist tried to show that all the countries were separate?

_____

_____

_____

By 1750, these four nations were controlled from London.

3. Look at the map on page 4. How has the artist tried to show that the countries were no longer separate?

_____

_____

_____

Nowadays, in the 1990s, only Eire is separate from the United Kingdom. However, a few people think that Scotland and Wales should have separate parliaments again. In Northern Ireland some people want to stay as part of the United Kingdom, whilst others want to join with Eire.

4. The third map you have is empty.

a) Label each country which makes up the United Kingdom.

b) Put your own symbols on the map to show which countries are still part of the United Kingdom.

c) Think of a way to show that they are all still governed from London.

d) Think of a way to show what some people in Scotland, Wales and Northern Ireland think about the situation.

The British Isles in 1500

The British Isles in 1750

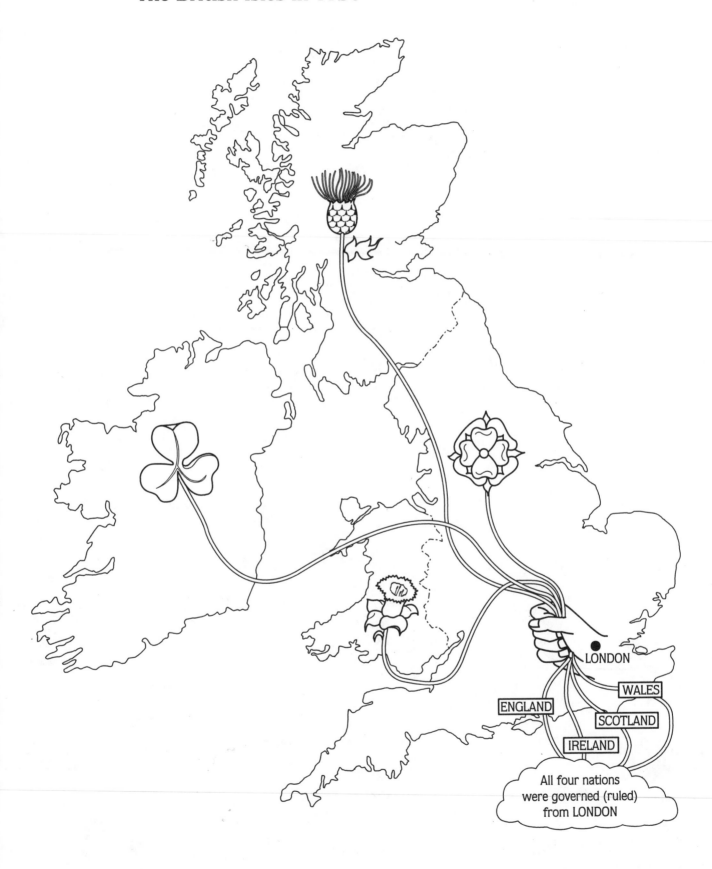

ENGLAND

WALES

SCOTLAND

IRELAND

LONDON

All four nations
were governed (ruled)
from LONDON

The British Isles in the 1990s

35

You will need

- scissors
- sheets of paper
- glue

Which country?

You should work in groups of three for this activity.

On pages 2, 3 and 4 are some cards. On each card you will find information about Ireland, Scotland or Wales.

Your task

1. Cut the cards out and sort them into three piles – cards about Ireland, Scotland and Wales.
2. Put each set of cards into chronological order.
3. Each person in the group chooses a set of cards with information about one country.
4. On a separate sheet of paper for each country, make a timeline for the events which took place in that country.
   - You could make a vertical timeline.
   - You could make a horizontal timeline.
   - You could copy all the information from the cards on to your timeline.
5. When you have finished your timelines, use them as part of a wall display showing how the countries became united to make the United Kingdom.
   - You could use the maps, flags and symbols.
   - You could use the timelines to help you to decide which were the most important events for each country.

1534
King Henry VIII argued with the Pope and the Catholic Church, but the Irish people stayed Catholic. They favoured the Pope, not King Henry.

1715
The Scots rebelled against the English but were defeated.

1638
There were riots in Scotland because King Charles had introduced an English prayer book. So the Scots invaded northern England.

1536
A law called the 'Act of Union' made Wales part of England.

1601
Irish Catholic rebels, helped by Spain, were defeated by Queen Elizabeth I. She took land off them and gave it to her Protestant supporters.

1543
A second law called the 'Act of Union' continued the process of making Wales part of England.

1549
A special edition of the Protestant prayer book was written for the Welsh in their own language.

1535

An Irish rebellion was stopped by the English.

1537

A law was passed forcing everyone in Ireland to speak English.

1745

Another Scottish rebellion was defeated.

1558

Mary Queen of Scots married the heir to the French throne.

1649

Oliver Cromwell ordered Catholics to be massacred (murdered) in Ireland.

1707

A law called the 'Act of Union' between England and Scotland was passed. They now shared the same parliament and government.

1560

The French king (Mary Queen of Scots' husband) died. Mary returned to Scotland where Protestant noblemen removed her from the throne.

1603	**1595**	**1587**
Mary Queen of Scots' son James, King of Scotland, became king of England as well. But England and Scotland kept their own parliaments and were still separate countries.	Catholic rebellions began in Ireland. 	Catholics plotted to make Mary Queen of Scots Queen of England in place of Elizabeth. The rebellion failed and Mary was beheaded. 
1689	**1641**	**1691**
English armies invaded Ireland. 	Irish Catholics rebelled against their English Protestant landlords. Houses were burned and people were murdered. 	The English army finally beat the Irish who had teamed up with the French. The loyal Protestant landowners (loyalists) were given their own parliament.
1650		
Irish Catholics lost their land. It was given to English Protestants. 		

History Dictionary

1. PEOPLE

citizen

A citizen was a rich merchant or craftsman who lived in a town. He had a large house and servants.

gentleman

A gentleman could be a rich duke or earl, who helped the king run the country. He was often an important landowner.

citizen's wife

A citizen's wife ran the household, hired servants, bought food and drink and organised the family's finances.

gentlewoman

Gentlewomen ran the household, hired servants and entertained guests invited by their husbands.

labourer

A labourer was someone who worked with his hands. He might work on a farm or in a town as a bricklayer or a shoemaker. He had no land of his own.

minister

A minister took **Protestant** Church services. Unlike a **Catholic** priest, he dressed very plainly.

labourer's wife

Labourers' wives had to help their husbands with their work as well as look after their families.

Parliamentarian

A parliamentarian was a person or soldier who supported Parliament during the English Civil War.

Pope

The Pope was head of the **Catholic** Church. He lived in Rome.

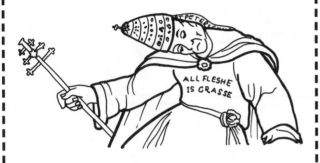

rogue

The government thought that some people had made themselves poor because they were too lazy to work. If they were caught begging they were punished. They were called rogues.

Puritan

A Puritan was a strict **Protestant** who believed in even simpler church services and a life devoted to God and other people. Puritans thought Sunday should be a holy day, and disapproved of dancing, gambling and other entertainments.

Royalist

A Royalist was a person or soldier who supported the King during the English Civil War.

vagrant

A vagrant was a very poor person who had no home or job. In the sixteenth and seventeenth centuries there were lots of vagrants who went round the country begging for food.

yeoman

A yeoman was a farmer who owned or rented land from a **gentleman**. He had quite a good life.

wet nurse

Rich mothers sent their babies to a wet nurse. She would feed and look after them until they were about eighteen months old.

yeoman's wife

Yeomen's wives helped their husbands on the farm. They looked after the vegetable gardens, chickens and goats, and were responsible for the cows and dairy produce.

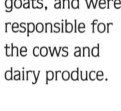

2. CONCEPTS AND TERMS

baptism
Baptism is when a baby is dipped in water in church and prayers are said for the baby by the priest. People believed you had to be baptised to go to heaven.

Bill of Mortality
A Bill of Mortality is a list showing how many people died and what they died of. For example it shows us how many people died of the plague in 1665.

British Isles
The British Isles is made up of England, Scotland, Wales, Northern Ireland and Eire.

Catholic
In 1500 England was still a Catholic country. People went to **mass**, paid **tithes** and believed they would go to hell if they were wicked and did not have their sins forgiven by the priest. Catholic churches were highly decorated and church services were given in Latin. The head of the Catholic Church was the **Pope**.

cause
A cause is a reason why something happens. For example, bad harvests were a cause of poverty in the sixteenth century.

civil war
A civil war is when people from the same country fight against each other.

confirmation
When you were about twelve years old you were confirmed. This gave you the power to fight the devil and be good. It made you a proper adult member of the **Catholic** Church.

consequence
A consequence is a result of something that happens. A consequence of bad harvests in the sixteenth century was that people did not have enough food.

the deserving poor
The government called a special group of poor people 'the deserving poor'. These might be children whose parents had died. The government gave these poor people a licence to beg for money and made other people pay **taxes** to help them.

dock
The dock is in a courtroom. It is where the person who is being tried for a crime has to stand while the judge hears what he has done.

execution
An execution happened when someone was found guilty of committing a crime and they were sentenced to death by the judge. They were then killed by the executioner.

feast
A feast is a large meal where there is lots of food and drink and music. It was often given to celebrate a wedding, a good harvest, or another happy event.

interpretation
An interpretation is how one person explains a historical event, or how he or she wants to show it, in a picture or in writing. Historians have to look at different interpretations of the same event.

last rites
The last rites were a kind of service given to you by the priest just before you died. This meant that when you died you would go to heaven.

Lord Protector
After King Charles I was beheaded Oliver Cromwell became ruler of the country and was known as the Lord Protector.

mass
Everyone went to church on Sunday to attend mass and take communion. This meant that they ate bread which was supposed to be the body of Jesus and drank red wine which was supposed to be his blood. They believed if you did not go to mass God would punish you.

nation
England, Scotland and Wales are separate nations which were joined together, with part of Ireland, to make the **United Kingdom**.

Parliament
Parliament was made up of representatives of the people. The king and Parliament ran the country.

plot
A plot is a secret plan, often thought up by two or more people.

Protestant
Protestants were given this name because they protested against the **Catholic** Church. For example, they said the Catholic Church was too rich and didn't give enough money to the poor. They also said that the Catholic priests were lazy and did not do their jobs properly. Protestants did not believe in **purgatory.**

purgatory
Catholics believed that purgatory was a place where most people were sent after they died. In purgatory they were punished for the things they had done wrong during their lives. The better Christian you had been, the less time you had to spend in purgatory. When you had been punished enough then you could go to heaven.

rebellion
A rebellion is when people stop obeying the king or government and openly fight against their control.

Reformation
In 1500 England had been a **Catholic** country. But by 1600 it was a **Protestant** country and there were no Catholic churches or priests left. This change was called the Reformation.

republic
A republic is a country which is governed without a king or queen. England was a republic after King Charles I was beheaded.

siege
A siege happens when there is a war or battle and a castle or town is surrounded by the enemy who are trying to get in.

tax
Tax was money people paid to the king or the Church.

tithe
A tithe was a special kind of tax that was paid to the Church. Everyone would give some of their money as it was a sin not to pay it.

treason
Treason is when someone goes against the king or state. If someone was found guilty of treason they would be sentenced to death.

trial
A trial happens when a person is thought to have committed a crime. At the trial the judge listens to evidence about what the person is supposed to have done and then the judge decides whether the person is guilty or innocent.

United Kingdom
The United Kingdom is made up of England, Scotland, Wales and Northern Ireland. It does not include Eire.

workhouse
Workhouses were set up by the government and towns to help the **deserving poor.**

THE MAKING OF THE UK SUPPORT MATERIALS

THE MAKING OF THE UK SUPPORT MATERIALS

NONSINE SOLE
IRIS.

13a
Picture Pack

13b
Picture Pack

Within image 13b, as part of the illustration:
PLATTE GRONDT des Verbrande Stadt LONDON

NIEUW MODELL om de afgebrande Stadt LONDON te HERBOUWEN

THE MAKING OF THE UK SUPPORT MATERIALS

ALTISSIMVS
CREAVIT DE TERRA MEDECYNAMET VIR
PRVDENS NON ABHOREBIT ILLAM
ANNO DOMMINI 1623

THE MAKING OF THE UK SUPPORT MATERIALS